Sleeping in
the Jungle

Sleeping in the Jungle

Elle B. Six

Book Design & Production • Columbus Publishing Lab
www.ColumbusPublishingLab.com

Copyright © 2020 by Elle B. Six

All rights reserved. This book, or parts thereof, may not be reproduced in any form without permission.

The author has tried to accurately recreate events, locales, and conversations from his memories. In order to maintain anonymity, in some instances the names of individuals and places may have been changed. In addition, some identifying characteristics and details such as physical properties, occupations, and places of residence may have been altered for the sake of privacy.

Paperback ISBN: 978-1-63337-355-6
E-Book ISBN: 978-1-63337-356-3
LCCN: 2019918124

Printed in the United States of America

Contents

PREFACE: Who I Was vs. Who I Am — 7

ONE: Like Father, Like Son — 9
TWO: The Party is Over — 19
THREE: Outsider — 28
FOUR: Run, Nigga, Run — 45
FIVE: The Jungle Gym — 57
SIX: Eighteen and Ready — 74
SEVEN: Sugar Hill — 80
EIGHT: Prom Night Massacre — 90
NINE: Drop Down — 102
TEN: Jerked My Life Away — 110
ELEVEN: The New Block — 141
TWELVE: I Do — 146
THIRTEEN: The Takeover — 154
FOURTEEN: See You Later — 165
FIFTEEN: Blind Letter — 175
SIXTEEN: Laugh to Keep from Crying — 192
SEVENTEEN: Politics Unusual — 201
EIGHTEEN: Blacker Than Black — 214
NINETEEN: Heavenly Plan — 222
TWENTY: Look out the Window — 235
TWENTY-ONE: Step of Obedience — 250
TWENTY-TWO: Hard to Say Goodbye — 256
TWENTY-THREE: Forgiveness — 266

*I am alive because of GOD'S AMAZING GRACE.
If only people knew how SWEET the sound of that grace truly is.
It has SAVED a wretch like me.*

*When you feel WORRIED that the devil seems to be scoring
all the points, remember that you already know
WHO IS GOING TO WIN THE GAME.*

Who I Was vs. Who I Am

PREFACE

I was homeless. I was abandoned. I was a drug dealer. I was a liar. I was a cheater. I was a convicted felon. I was a drug addict. I was a sex addict. I was a thief. I was a coward. I was an absentee father. I was an imperfect husband. I was Karma.

But now:

I am a writer. I am a filmmaker. I am a scholar. I am an investor. I am baptized. I am an inspiration. I am saved. I am anointed. I am God's most precious belonging.

If you were to ask me if I were any of these labels, the truthful answer would be yes. But before I was any of these things, *I was just the boy sleeping in the jungle gym.*

Like Father, Like Son
SUMMER 1991

Brrrrrring, brrrrring. "Pop, wake up—the doorbell." *Brrrrrring, brrrrring.* "Come on, Pop. It's customers at the door." I gently shook him and hit the button on the intercom system wired from the bed to the front door. "Who is it?"

"Breeze and friends," a deep voice replied. I knew my father would be upset if he missed an opportunity to make some money, but he'd drank so much whiskey waiting on people to arrive that he was passed out drunk.

I shook him again. "Come on, Pop. Get up!" I heard someone mention over the intercom that they should leave, so I pushed the button again. "On my way down." Even though it was nearly midnight, I thought, *The hell with it!* I decided to let them in to have a seat at the bar. When somebody played the jukebox and the sounds of the party began, my dad would surely wake up. Unlocking the door, I saw the dark, muscled Cool Breeze and three strangers. "What's going on, Cool Breeze?"

"What's up, youngster? Where yo daddy?"

"He's upstairs but he'll be down in a minute."

Breeze walked in with three girls and another gentleman and yelled at the top of his lungs, "Hey Hickey, I got these hoes down here!" The group walked through the living room covered in booger-green carpet that hosted a jukebox, three brown metal tables, and twelve chairs. Breeze gave one of the girls two quarters to play the jukebox, and everyone else walked into the kitchen where the bar was located.

The bar was where customers congregated the most. The bar took up most of the kitchen. It was made of a polished brown cedar wood that hosted every liquor imaginable underneath. There was a large cabinet that rose up the wall behind the bar that kept your store essentials. Pickles, gum, potato chips, sausages, cigarettes, basically anything to satisfy a customer in an after-hours establishment.

I walked in behind everyone, made my way behind the bar, and threw a white towel over my shoulder. "What can I get you ladies?"

Before any of the ladies could answer, the guy who accompanied them blurted out, "How old is you, boy?"

"Do you mean how old *are* you? I'm fifteen years old and this is 1991, so *wees* don't have to talk like slaves no mo, sir!"

Everybody in the room burst out laughing. I was the worst person in the world to give an audience to, so if this guy wanted to embarrass me in front of these ladies, he was going to be in for a long night.

"We ain't gettin' ready to buy no drinks from no fifteen-year-old punk." Breeze tried to grab his friend, but it was too late.

"First of all, I asked the ladies if they wanted a drink. I ain't ask you shit. And if you ain't gonna buy no drink from me, them big-ass lips gonna be so dry, if you smile you gon' crack 'em and bleed to death." The fact was: this brother's lips *were* huge. Breeze and all three ladies were grabbing their stomachs, laughing. "On second thought, I can't have them big-ass lips bleeding on the floor. Here, have a drink on the house."

By this time, even the guy with big lips was laughing.

Sleeping in the Jungle

My plan worked! All the commotion finally woke my father, but he wasn't pleased. He would never have permitted me to open the door when he was asleep because of the security risk. "What the fuck is this, son?" he whispered in my ear as he stood behind me, trying to play it cool in front of the customers.

"We couldn't miss this money simply because you were too drunk to wake up. Breeze is a regular, and I knew he was bringing you some new girls for you to pimp. I figured the commotion would wake you up…and it did. Now look at these hoes. Ain't you glad I didn't let them get away?"

He scanned the room, then just looked back at me and laughed. "Hell yeah!" We hugged and prepared for a great night. "Son, take the ladies upstairs and show them their rooms."

Leading the ladies out of the kitchen into the living room where the jukebox was playing, I turned and said, "I'm sorry, I didn't catch your names."

And in order, one behind the other, they said, "I'm Tesha," "Diane," and "Cat." Tesha was tall, very slender, light-brown skin, little to no breasts, ass was nonexistent, but she wore her early forty years quite well. Diane was short and regular; nothing too memorable about her at all. Now Cat, that was a different set of circumstances. Cat might have been one of the prettiest girls who'd ever entered my father's joint. Many prostitutes came and went, but none like her. I was 5'2" and she stood eye to eye with me. I understood why they called her Cat; her eyes were identical to a feline's. Light-brown skin, ideal B-cup breasts, perfectly round ass. This unbelievable beauty was in her late twenties but could've passed as a teenager. She looked that young.

"Diane and Tesha, this is your room. Cat, your room is across the hall." My father taught me to always put the prettiest girl in a room by herself, because she'd get the most business. He had his reasons for having her in a room by herself, and I had mine. I had first dibs on that ass.

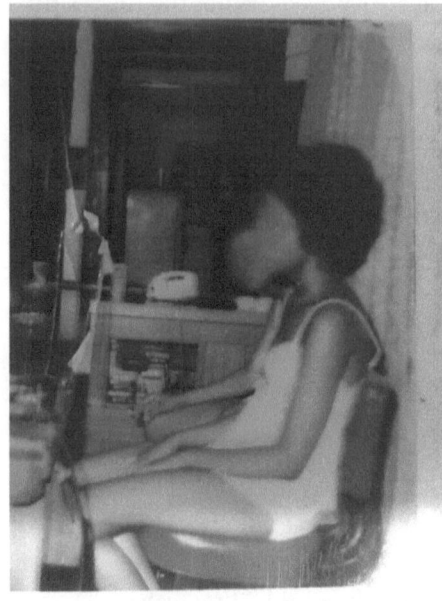
Ladies of the night

•••

My dad was one of the ambassadors of pimpin' women. He had one philosophy: "All these hoes really want is something to eat."

I carried up a plate of sausage and pancakes to Cat's room at seven o'clock the next morning. By the time she took the last bite, I could feel her looking at me seductively. I had already undressed her with my eyes, so it was good to see that we were on the same page. Pop's formula worked quite marvelously! Cat slid over, pulled my jogging shorts down, and went to work. I usually had to work my charm to get one of Pop's girls to forget that sleeping with a fifteen-year-old was a felony, but this one needed no convincing.

Although I'd had sex many times before with different women of the house, Cat was taking me places I'd never gone. Only in the movies would you see a girl so freaked out. It was unbelievable. I screamed, "Oh my God!" At that moment, I knew I was in love.

It was difficult having feelings for Cat while watching her be a woman of the night. She had sex with anybody who had forty bucks and gave oral sex to anyone for twenty. The unfortunate part of her being so beautiful was that every man seemed to choose her. Even though I saw her working through the night, I still had sex with her every day.

SLEEPING IN THE JUNGLE

I hated seeing her in that type of work, because she meant a lot to me. She had been in the house for nearly three months, and the longer she stayed, the more she became like family. It was more than just a sexual thing; we watched movies together, played games, cracked jokes, and really enjoyed each other's company. I tried to teach her how the business was run, how to hide the money, and how to attract new girls. Attracting new girls was essential to keeping the business running, because we were always losing girls. The house was a revolving door, but not for Cat. She was a star.

"You're either an old man pretending to be a teenage boy, or a young genius."

"I'm not an old man or a genius. I just know the hoe business from the best teacher in the world, my dad."

Every now and then you ran across a smooth-talking pimp who made his way into your establishment looking to recruit new girls. One night there was some light-skinned pretty-looking jerk whispering

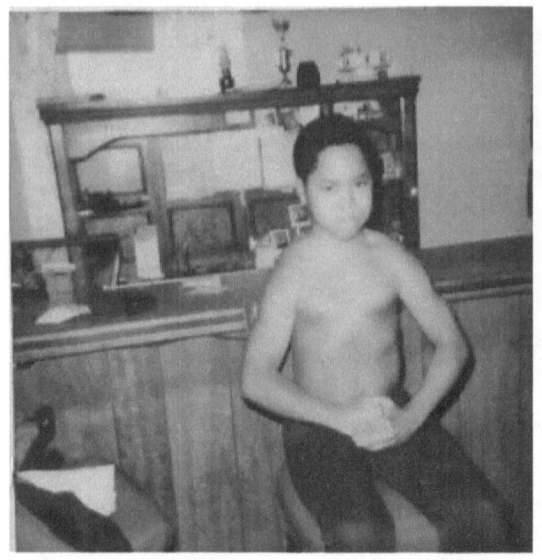

in Cat's ear for over an hour. I had my eyes fixed on them while I was making drinks, because it seemed like she was falling for his game a little too hard. I'd been staring at them so long that I didn't even realize that my dad was standing in the doorway. She must have felt him standing there, because she turned around by the power of his glare. Once their eyes met, I knew there was trouble.

My dad took two steps toward her and pulled a knife out of his back pocket. He swung it toward her neck, stopping just short of cutting her. Everyone in the bar held their breath as they watched the scene unfold.

"What did I do, Daddy?" she asked as her voice cracked with extreme nervousness and her eyes watered with guilt.

Her question went unanswered and he slowly moved the knife down her neck, down her body, stopping just above her breast, and he quickly cut her bra strap. Cat sat there with her breast exposed, and a folded-up hundred-dollar bill fell to the floor.

"I was going to tell you about that, Daddy."

"You can't tell me about it after I know about it." My dad turned and shook hands with the guy who was sweet-talking Cat. "Thanks, Ted."

"Anytime, Hickey," he said as he got up and left the bar.

Cat jumped out of her chair and ran up the stairs in embarrassment.

My dad had seemed angry at the time, but he was surprisingly calm now. We went on partying through the night as if nothing had happened.

Wow, it was a test, I thought. A test she'd failed miserably. My dad had that guy come in there to sweet-talk Cat to see if she was loyal. I wasn't sure what the repercussions of her actions would be, but she would have to do a lot to make things right with my dad. My heart was beating out of my chest because I knew this was bad. I just hoped it wasn't bad enough to lose her. I would've done anything in my power to help her fix this.

This was one night that the party outlasted my stamina, so I decided to go to bed early. Even though I'd quickly gone to sleep, I snapped awake to the sound of screaming. *What the hell is going on?* I jumped out of the bed and opened the door to the sight of my dad standing over Cat, holding a belt. My body froze with surprise and fear at what was unfolding in front of me.

"Bitch, you tried to steal from me? Huh?"

"No, Daddy, I swear I was gon' tell you about the money."

"Shut up, hoe," he said as he swung the belt and struck her.

"Aaaaagh, I'm sorry, Daddy." She tried to crawl away.

I ran down the hallway and grabbed my dad from behind. "Dad, stop, she's sorry."

My dad slung his arms backward out of pure adrenaline and threw me across the room. I flew back against the wall and was instantly dazed. The pain from hitting the wall was like a lightning bolt shot through my head. Woozy but still aware, I ran back over to the commotion and grabbed my dad again more forcefully. "Dad, no! Leave her alone."

This time, my dad was aware of what I was doing and quickly turned his attention toward me. He slowly walked in my direction, put his forearm against my chest, and slammed me against the wall. The pressure of his arm was so powerful that I could hardly take a breath. "Boy, don't you ever in your life challenge me over one of these hoes. You think she cares about you because she gave you a little pussy? Don't you trust these hoes, son. Don't you ever trust these hoes." As my father walked away, I stood there, stunned, as he left me with a parting message. "Why don't you take your thieving hoe in the room and see if she wants to give you some pussy one last time? When you're done, tell your bitch to pack her shit and get the fuck out."

Although my dad left the hallway, I still stood there glued to the wall as I glared at Cat on the floor crying. Her hair was a mess, her makeup was smeared, and her clothes were stretched and torn. "Why did you do this, Cat? I thought you loved me?"

"I do love you. Please talk to your dad and convince him to let me stay. I'll do anything. You want me to come in your room and make it up to you?"

Right there in that moment, I knew my dad was right. She was playing me. She was a beautiful woman who thought she could get men to do anything by offering sex. I loved her, but I would not be played. "Naw, I don't want anything from you. You heard my dad. Get your shit and get the fuck out of here." I walked away as she looked at me with regret, tears all over her face. I eased into my room and slowly started closing the door, but not without a final parting word before slamming the door. "BITCH."

•••

The next morning was extremely awkward without Cat in the house. I didn't want to get out of bed because I was afraid of what my dad would say about last night. The strange thing was that I missed Cat already. She could have very well been my first love. Before I could put some thought into what I would say to my dad, I heard the door creak open.

"Hey son, are you awake?"

"Yeah, Pop, I'm up."

"Come on out here for a second, because I want to talk to you."

Damn! I sure hope he's not mad at me. I began to tremble. "Okay, Pop, I'll be out in a second." As I walked out of the room, I didn't know what to expect, so I just prepared myself for anything. I made my way down to the living room and saw my dad sitting at the table.

"Sit down, son. I want to apologize for what happened last night."

"No need to apologize to me, Dad. I understand."

"No, son, hear me out and don't interrupt. I exposed you to the ugly side of what I do, and sometimes I forget how young you are. I know how you feel about Cat, and I was wrong for the way I reacted. I need you to understand that in this business, weakness can destroy you. If you allow one person to steal, ten people will steal. I love having you as my right-hand man because you're my son and you're the only person I can trust. I need you to promise me two things, son. First, promise me that no matter what you do, you'll stay in school. Let me hear you promise me."

"Of course I'll stay in school, Dad. I promise."

"Second, no matter if you're a criminal or a doctor, always know that when you're in trouble, you can call on the Lord. I know my life doesn't always reflect it, but my momma instilled that into all of her kids. The Lord is your father just like I'm your father. There is nothing He wouldn't do for His child. You're special, David! I see something different in you that I've never seen in any person. It may be because you're my son, but I choose to believe that you have a great destiny to fulfill. Bow your head with me, and let's pray.

"Dear Father, we come to you today with a heavy heart. Thank you for forgiving us when we do things that are wrong. Thank you for blessing and keeping Cat and giving her your favor on her journey. Thank you for your shield of protection, and help us to be better. Thank you for reading our hearts. Thank you for your grace. Thank you for your mercy. Thank you for using our lives for good instead of the way that we live now. Because you're not here to show us the way, Lord, we thank you for forgiving us for being lost. Although it may be too late for me, I thank you for using David's life to be great. Thank you that no weapon formed against him will ever prosper. We thank you for this and all things, in your son Jesus Christ's name, Amen."

"Wow, Pop, that was deep."

"You're supposed to say 'amen' also."

"Oh. Amen. Why is it that we never prayed together before?"

"I don't know, but it was overdue. I tossed and turned all night last night in guilt over the way I behaved in front of you, and God told me I needed to teach you about Him. To be quite honest, I never prayed like that before. Maybe it's a new beginning for the both of us."

I'd never seen my dad that emotional and sincere. He was usually so rough, hard, and angry. I liked this side of my dad. As I sat and replayed my thoughts over the promises I'd made my dad about school and prayer, I felt his hand reach under my armpit to raise me from my chair. Out of all the things I didn't expect this morning, that was the most unexpected. My dad embraced me in a vise-like hug that pushed all the oxygen out of my young lungs. Every time I exhaled, I had difficulty inhaling because the hug was so tight.

The Party is Over

Sunday was always a somber day. I lived with my mom during the weekdays to attend school, but I spent the weekends and the entire summer hustling with my father. My mom may have had the best single mother situation in the world. Dad took me with him every weekend and the entire summer; that was sweet. She knew nothing about my life at Dad's. Plus, I loved living the double life. It was exciting.

I attended school at the Ohio School of Science. I achieved pretty good grades, but I got into trouble a lot for being the class clown.

One autumn day, I came in from school and saw my mom crying at the dinner table. "What's wrong, Ma?"

"Come over here and sit down, baby. You're going to have to go and live with your father for a little while, because I have to check myself into a drug rehabilitation center."

"What… Why?"

"I'm addicted to crack, son," she confessed shamefully.

"What the hell is crack, and why can't you just stop using it?" I crossed my arms so tight that it was cutting off my circulation. The anger seared as my eyes squinted to the point that it seemed as if I was looking through her. I loved my mother so much. She was the strongest lady I knew. If anyone could beat this, she could. When I thought about the fact that I spent every weekend and all summer with my dad, I began to realize I didn't really know my mother that well. She represented the clean and wholesome side of my life, and my father represented the street life. Now that the street life had infiltrated the wholesome side of my life, nothing seemed sacred anymore. Everything felt tainted.

Why is this happening to her? I didn't totally understand, because there was only so much she would share, but I guessed I could put up with my father's partying lifestyle during the week.

•••

As the weeks passed, I couldn't wait for my mom to get home from rehab. Listening to the jukebox blaring all night when I had to go to school the next morning was unbearable. I was so tired in class that I could hardly stay awake. I loved my dad, but I missed my mom more than words could say. She provided stability and balance, regardless of her crack addiction. I needed a break from living with my father.

Before I knew it, I was saying, "Welcome home, Mama!" Luckily her stint in rehab only took three months. I had never been so happy to see my mom. I didn't realize how well I had it living with her during the week. Although she only stood 4'11", her attitude was 6' tall! She did her best to give me the best life that she could. Life with her was calm. After all, who could live every day in an after-hours bar? My dad was the only person built for that. The parties never started until the legal bars closed. I thanked God that things returned to normal. Mom got back on track working, and coupled with the financial help from my dad, I never wanted for anything.

•••

Sleeping in the Jungle

Over the next year, my father and I became partners in crime. I took care of the bar and the girls, and he took care of the drug front. A one-stop shop. My dad sold women, pills, weed, codeine syrup, cocaine, alcohol, sodas, sausages, gum, chicken dinners, etc. If you wanted it, he had it, all in one house. I'd always looked down on drug addicts as inferior human beings until my mom had her experience with addiction. She humanized addicts to a certain extent for me and made it difficult to judge them as harshly when they came to the house.

Our entire kitchen was configured like a bar in a nightclub. If you ate a meal, you sat at the bar. If you ate in the living room, you were next to a jukebox. As the business grew more successful, my father became paranoid. Having a house on a dead-end street underneath the Kinsman Bridge was both a gift and a curse. A gift, because you had privacy when running an illegal business, but a curse if something went wrong and there were no neighbors to call the police. Three blocks separated his house and the Garden Valley Projects. He always kept a gun on him, even when naked. He only took the gun off to bathe or have sex.

Another Friday arrived. I was supposed to go to my dad's, but I felt horrible. I couldn't function at school, and my insides were in knots. "Hey, Mama," I said, walking in from school.

"What's wrong, baby?" she asked as if she could see the illness in my eyes.

"I don't feel good," I muttered in pure duress.

"Aw, poor baby. I'm going to call your dad and tell him you're staying home this weekend."

This would be my first time missing a Friday night at my father's house in years. As bad as I felt, I was happy to stay right where I was, because nobody could nurse me back to health like my mommy. I was so sick that I couldn't stop shaking. I whispered into the air, "What the hell is wrong with me?"

As the clock struck midnight, I shook violently, my muscles kept contracting, and my stomach felt like I'd done a million sit-ups. *Am I dying?* I didn't have a cold, I wasn't throwing up—just nonstop trembling. At about 4:00 a.m., just as I felt as if I couldn't take it anymore, the shaking stopped. The physical fatigue of what I'd experienced wouldn't allow me to celebrate the fact that my shaking had finally stopped. I felt my head falling toward the pillow into a state of deep sleep.

● ● ●

"Holy crap," I said with a big smile as I woke up the next day. I felt 100 percent normal. In fact, I felt like a million bucks!

With this revelation, I called my dad so he could come get me for the Saturday night festivities. The phone rang nonstop but there was no answer. An hour later—no answer. Call after call, and I hadn't gotten an answer all day. That wasn't like him, because he couldn't stay away from his house too long. The house *was* his business.

I voiced my concerns to my mom. "Something's wrong," I said as I began crying, pacing, and refusing to relent.

"If we don't hear from him by morning, we'll see what's going on. You know your daddy. He's okay."

The sun came up the next day, and I was extremely worried. "Can you take me to Dad's?" I pleaded. Eighty-third and Kinsman was a mere fifteen-minute drive from where we lived on 142nd and Harvard. What the hell was the problem? I could clearly see that my mom was stalling because she had something on her mind, but I had no idea what it could be.

"Ma, why ain't you taking me? Wait…why are you crying? What's wrong?"

I yelled in disbelief as she explained that my dad was dead. He'd been found face-down in a pool of blood with one bullet to the back of his head and one in the chest. She'd just received the call with the grim news but couldn't figure out how to tell me.

"No," I screamed as I ran down the stairs. I grabbed the door frantically to run outside and felt a tugging grasp from behind. My mother swiftly spun my head around and held me in a loving hug.

So many thoughts ran through my mind. *He'd been heavily armed. Who could have killed him? Who? Could it be that he'd known his killer? Why hadn't I been there? Wait, I should have been there. Oh yeah, the phantom, unexplained illness that had left me bedridden through the night had prevented me from going. Was I shaking so violently because I'd felt my dad's fear? Had I shaken because I'd felt the bullets as they'd ripped through my best friend? When the shaking had suddenly stopped, was that the moment my father had died? Could I have saved him, or would I have been lying next to him in the morgue?*

Wait a second, did the phantom illness save my life? If that's true, then that means there's a higher power. Right? No way. I don't believe that for a second. I don't even go to church. If the Lord stepped in to save me, then that would mean He has a plan for my life. But why would the Lord choose me? Who am I?

Momma What?

Wow, this is real. My mom told me my father was dead, but it didn't really sink in until I saw all the police cars surrounding his house.

"Mom, pull over." I jumped out of the car as we drove up to my dad's house. I ran up to the house, but the police wouldn't let me past the yellow tape surrounding the scene. As the police moved to restrain me, I felt an embrace from the rear. I turned around and saw it was my Uncle Craig. He'd found his brother on the second floor, dead from two gunshot wounds. The pain in his eyes displayed every emotion. He was in shock at the sight of finding his brother slain. He feared what would come of my young life now that my dad was gone. He was angry at the killers. Most importantly, I saw my uncle's sense of loss. My dad was the only person who'd ever hugged me this tightly. As much as I wanted to tell him to release me, I needed the comfort of the squeeze.

"Oh my God!" I said when the paramedics wheeled my father's lifeless body out of the house. The white sheet that covered his body on the fast-moving gurney was soaked in blood from a gaping head wound. I was unable to turn away because my body was paralyzed with shock. I watched with horror when they loaded his body into the ambulance. As the ambulance pulled away, I kept waiting on the doors to somehow fly open and my dad to leap out. I always thought that my dad was Superman! How could Superman be dead? Nobody could kill him!

Lord, please help me…

The Black Eye

As I walked into the funeral home to finally see my dad's body before the funeral, my stomach was in knots and I was one burp away from vomiting. I was with my mom and Aunt Sadie. *Who could have murdered my best friend?* This was going to be the first time I'd seen my dad's face since he'd died. However, I didn't have an overwhelming sense of grief. There was a sense of relief at replacing the sight of him being wheeled out of the house in a bloody bedsheet. The perfect substitute for the horrific vision would be the sight of him styled in a well-pressed suit and ready to meet the Lord.

Although I was relieved at the thought of getting a better vision of my father, I would've done anything to get out of going to this funeral. I didn't want to look at my father lying in a casket and watch people walk past him saying the same bullshit words:

"He sure does look good."

"He looks like he died in his sleep."

It would seem somewhat sincere if twenty-five people didn't come up and tell you the same thing. At least my dad could look good one more time. I'd picked out the finest suit I could find. My dad loved to look good. I considered it my obligation to make sure his home-going would make him proud.

As the casket was opened, I closed my eyes. Although they were shut, I was listening intently. I heard the gasps and crying from my mom and Aunt Sadie. When calm finally presented itself with a hum of quiet, I slowly opened my eyes so I could give my reaction on how good he looked. "Who the hell is that?" I screamed at the funeral director.

"What do you mean, son?"

"That's not my father. That's not my father." I stepped backward and fought off tears.

"How can you show us the wrong bo—" I squinted my eyes; I looked a little closer. "Holy crap. That is my father, but why is he so dark?"

"Yeah, why is he so dark?" Aunt Sadie added with both anger and curiosity in her face.

Unsure how to answer with heated questions coming in rapid succession, the funeral director slowly began to hang his head. "He's so dark because he died on his knees bending over, and all the blood rushed to his face."

"OH MY GOD, WHY?" Aunt Sadie screamed.

Everyone was taking the news so terribly that no one even saw me slip out of the room. *Wow, execution style!* I walked to the parking lot and envisioned every movie I'd ever seen with an execution-style murder. As my eyes welled with tears, I knew these weren't just tears of grief. These were also tears of relief that death had come fast. Everybody was making such a big deal about the fact that he was so dark, nobody noticed the fact that he had a perfectly round black eye. I mean, this was a black eye that could have been delivered by Mike Tyson. My father was a very good-looking man. There was no way he would've wanted people staring at him all beat up.

"Insensitive prick," I whispered as I thought about the funeral director who'd said my dad had died on his face. Did anybody think the fifteen-year-old son might have needed to leave the room before he said that?

The only thing I knew was that my dad would've wanted to look good and I couldn't even deliver that—I'd failed him. I was so embarrassed for him!

Watching people enter the funeral home, I remembered that I'd been dreading the same old statements: "*He sure does look good.*" "*He looks like he died in his sleep.*"

Now I would give anything to have someone say one of those. *Please, somebody say it. Anybody?* I couldn't even grieve my dad at his funeral, because all I could do was watch everybody's reactions when they saw him for the first time after his death. *Why did he have to have a black eye?* People must have been mortified by his appearance.

Good News/Bad News

It was just days before the funeral, and even though it was a sad time, we received some good news. They'd caught the people who'd murdered my dad. When the intruders kicked in the door, my father shot one of them. It was the intruder's injuries that ultimately led to his capture. After realizing the severity of his crimes, he'd quickly told on his co-conspirators. His confession was how the police were able to apprehend all of the perpetrators. It was just like my dad to have one of his final actions be what solved his own murder. There were seven intruders in total, and although I was saddened by the number of people my father had had to face in his last hours, I was inspired that it would take that many people to defeat Superman.

My entire family was sitting around the TV as the police made the arrests public. *Hell yeah, they got all those bastards.* They paraded each one of the intruders in front of the camera. I was surprised to see that one of them was a female.

"Oh my God! No, it can't be? Is that…Cat?" I tried to swallow but there was no saliva in my mouth. The heat turned up in my face as if I were in a pressure cooker, and I slowly began to struggle to take in a single breath.

Oh no, I can't believe Cat was involved in this. I thought she loved me! All the times she'd been talking to me, befriending me, and ultimately making love to me had just been a ploy to get information from me. I'd trusted her so much that she'd become like family. She'd used me and I'd been such a fool for her. I'd told her things about my dad that no one knew. I'd entrusted her with the information about where the money was. *Oh no, it was my fault!* I'd gotten my father killed by running my mouth. Even though I was only fifteen, I knew better! My dad had told me never to trust these women, and this was why.

I screamed in pain as everyone turned to look at me with surprise. My scream put an instant end to the high fives and jubilee everyone was experiencing. As I cried and ran out of the house, no one knew why I was hysterical. Stumbling down the street, reeling in tears and pain, I quickly concluded I would never tell anyone what I'd done. I'd take this secret to my grave. I was the one who'd gotten my dad killed. How would I ever live with myself? *I'm so sorry, Dad!* My heart pounded as if it were outside my chest. My mind raced as guilt settled in every part of my soul. *How could I be so stupid?*

Outsider

It was nearly six months after my dad's funeral, and reality began to set in. I came to realize that my mom and I didn't know each other at all. Even though I'd lived with her during the week, we'd never spent any real time together. I went to school during the day while she was at work. After school I'd come home, do my homework, then hurry outside to play with my friends. I returned home when the streetlights came on, had dinner, and watched TV until I went to sleep. On Fridays, my father would pick me up and I wouldn't return until Monday. I'd just lost my father, yet I couldn't help feeling that she didn't want me there.

Now that my dad wasn't there to contribute financially, and there was so much bureaucracy in getting the Social Security checks coming, Mom was as irritable as ever.

"What's up, Ma? Everything okay?"

"No baby, everything is not okay. We have to move into the upstairs house over Grandma until we get on our feet."

"Momma, no!" First my dad, then living above Grandma's. I loved my grandmother dearly, but she didn't like me at all. Nothing I ever did was right in her eyes, and living upstairs from her would be a nightmare.

Sleeping in the Jungle

My grandmother was born in southern Alabama in the 1920s. She was no-nonsense, no fun, no humor. Kids should not speak when adults were speaking, and you didn't even think about making eye contact during discipline. I wouldn't say she had a slave mentality, but she was definitely old school. She was also a double amputee. She'd lost both of her legs to gangrene. She was confined to a wheelchair but somehow made her way to every window and door. She had very strict rules that weren't typical of most grandmothers: *Don't ask to go anywhere. Don't ask to go in my refrigerator. Don't ask me for anything.* In the fifteen years I'd been alive, she'd never bought me one thing. No birthdays, no Christmas—nothing ever. Life just seemed to keep sinking lower and lower.

It took about a week, but we finally got everything moved into the upstairs over Grandma. She owned a two-family house on the east side of Cleveland, and somebody from the family always lived above her. Now I guess it was our turn. It was a nice-sized unit and just as cozy as the single-family house we'd lived in. The only downside was Grandma. She could never see you sitting around with nothing to do. The moment she spotted you relaxing, she gave you a chore. I was just going to stay out of her sight, do my homework, and listen to music. Everything in my life had been downgraded over the last six months. I went from the kid who'd had the latest clothes and shoes to the bum who couldn't even muster up decent school clothes for the upcoming school year. All I wanted to do was sit in my room and listen to my radio.

As soon as I grabbed the small silver boom box, I noticed somebody had broken the antenna. *What the hell?* The only thing I enjoyed was my radio. How could somebody just break my stuff and try to stick it back down in the hole like I wasn't going to notice?

"David," my grandmother yelled from downstairs.

"Yes, Grandma?"

"Come here."

"Okay."

"*Fuck*," I whispered under my breath. I knew this would be some bullshit by the way she yelled my name. I could always tell when she wasn't in a good mood. "Hey, Grandma." I kissed her on the cheek as I sat down.

"David, I have to talk to you about something. I just found out your mother has been receiving your Social Security check for the past three months without telling us."

"*What?*"

"They also paid her a lump sum check that dated back to when your father died."

How could she do me like that? I looked down at my hand and I realized I was still holding the broken radio antenna. "That's it! I'll bet you she's back smoking crack, Grandma." Metal radio antennas could double as crack pipes because of their frame and durability. If she was using my antenna to smoke crack, then the rest of the antenna would be hidden somewhere in her bedroom.

I ran up the stairs with my heart racing as I burst into her bedroom. I knew she wouldn't be returning from work for several hours. "Where is it?" I muttered as I swiped through her nightstand. Drawers? Empty. Closets? Empty. *If she has it, it'll be close.* I lifted the mattress, only to see what I didn't want to see. The antenna! It was wrapped in tape at one end with black residue burned into it at the other end. *When is it going to stop? When is my low point going to reach bottom? What the hell am I going to do?*

Hustler's Birth

"Look, Grandma! I told you what it had to be, and when she gets home, I'm going to confront her."

Sleeping in the Jungle

"Hold on now. You're going to stay in a child's place."

"Okay, Grandma," I said in submission, but there was no way I was going to let this slide.

I paced back and forth waiting on my mother to get home, slowly working myself into a rage. My eyes were bloodshot red, and every word I rehearsed was through a set of clenched teeth. How could she do that to me? My father had just been murdered six months ago. *She doesn't give a damn about me! Wait until she gets home...* Better yet, I knew what I could tell her for breaking her promise of never smoking crack again. I could tell her I was leaving. Yeah, that was it. I knew this would bring her to her knees for sure. She would never go back to using crack if I hit her with that one. Suddenly my anxiety subsided. My plan was surefire. I could hardly wait!

"What's up, Ma?" I said with a sarcastic, smug smile as she entered our front door that evening. "Welcome home."

Curious but caught off guard at my tone, she said, "What do you mean by that?"

"I found your little crack pipe that you made from my antenna. How could you break my stuff so you could get high?"

That was when I woke up the little giant. "Break your stuff? Everything in this house is mine!"

Arguing with my mother was foreign territory. I had never and would never disrespect my mother in any way. I was unsure how far to go, but I'd picked the battle so I was ready to finish it. "My father bought me that radio."

Before I could finish my statement, I heard, "David! GET YO ASS DOWN HERE."

"NAW, GRANDMA, SHE NEEDS TO HEAR THIS." I was puffed up with boldness as I entered unchartered waters. "My father just got shot in the head and you want to run around getting high? What about me? You've been lying, saying they haven't sent the money for my dad yet, and you've spent it on dope. That's my money."

As soon as the words left my lips, she pounced on them. "Your money? Are you paying rent? Lights? Gas? Your father didn't just leave you, he left us!"

"Well I'm the only one who seems to be broken up about it! The only one mourning! You just took all the money for yourself and left me taking a beating. You know what, Mama? You don't have to worry about me no more. If you want to get high, then get high." I walked out the back door and stopped in the middle landing just as my mother stepped out behind me. "I'm leaving!"

I stared at her. It was like somebody had just stolen her pride. I knew this would break her down, and a part of me felt sorry for her, but she needed to learn a lesson.

Just like I thought, she turned to speak. She whispered small sounds in the softest, calmest, and smoothest voice she'd ever used. "Okay, bye!"

BOOM! The door slammed in my face.

I walked down the street toward Harvard Avenue and whispered, "Okay, bye? What the hell does she mean, 'Okay, bye'?" I had never factored in the fact that I didn't have anywhere to go. A part of me thought she'd say, "Don't go. I'm sorry. I'll get clean. I love you." Anything but, "Okay, bye." What the hell was I going to do now? The only person in my family I trusted was my cousin Dee. *Yeah, I'll call Dee.* He was one of my mother's nephews, but got respect as the patriarch of the family after my grandfather had died. He'd been in the military and was one of the only accomplished members of the family. He was the only one to finish high school. He was also the first one to attend college, and in our family, your respect was usually dictated by how many possessions you had. My cousin had cars, houses, and nice clothes. So that pretty much made him the man!

I slammed a quarter into a payphone. "What's up, Dee?"

"Who is this?"

"It's David."

"David, how you holding up, boy? I heard about your dad."

My eyes welled with tears to the point that my vision was so blurry I couldn't see. I choked back the tears, but my voice still carried sorrow. "Can you please come pick me up?"

"Why, what's wrong?"

"Come on, man, don't make me have to explain on this payphone. Just come get me." After thirty minutes, I finally saw him coming down the street. Not only did I see him, I heard him, too. The loud music coming from his car felt like a minor earthquake.

"What's up, cousin? Get in."

We slapped hands. "I have to know what kind of speakers you got back there. I heard you all the way down the street."

"You ain't got to worry about that. Let me just blow yo eardrums out." *BOOM PA CHA. BOOM BOOM PA CHA.*

I wanted to tell him to turn the music down so I could spill my heart out, but I couldn't escape the great feeling of having everyone turn their heads to look at the car where I was prominently riding in the front seat. I felt terrible and I had no idea what my next move was, but at that moment I felt like a hood star. We pulled over to the curb in front of a house I didn't recognize, and I noticed a guy running out of the driveway toward us.

As he got to the window out of breath, he said, "What's up, Dee? I got four hundred."

Suddenly Dee opened a compartment in his dashboard and pulled out the biggest bag of dope I'd ever seen in my life. I was trying my best to maintain my composure as if this were normal, but my heart was pumping so fast that I felt like I was about to have a seizure. "Here you go, playa." Dee handed him some drugs and quickly sped off.

"Damn, cuz, you're riding awfully dirty to be out for a stroll beating music. You gotta let me out of this hot-ass car."

He burst out laughing. "What the hell you know about a car being hot, lil' nigga?"

"I know everything about a hot car, and I can tell you everything about hustling. I can tell you everything that just took place with your boy," I said cockily.

"Okay, fourteen-year-old know-it-all nigga, hit me with it."

"He had four hundred dollars, right?"

"Yup."

"Now, you're either the most expensive game in town if you sold him a quarter ounce for four hundred, or you're the cheapest game in town if you sold him a half ounce for four hundred. And if you sold him a half ounce for four hundred, I'm gonna need one of them myself!"

Dee was laughing so hard that he almost crashed the car.

"I don't need one now, but I need one right now, shit."

"Stop it, Dave, for real. Be quiet, man. I have to drive this car." Although he was laughing at me, he was also staring at me with amazement. "Where the hell did you learn about selling dope wit' yo young ass?"

"Me and my father used to sell dope together." This was a complete lie, but who the hell was he going to ask, my dad? "Yeah, at his after-hours joint. We were a team." As he turned onto my street, I blurted out, "No, cuz, don't take me home."

"Why?"

"Because I caught my mother getting high and I walked out without even thinking about what I was going to do next. I called you because I need a place to go, and if you let me come stay with you, maybe we can be a team too. Come on, man, you can trust me. All I need is a place to stay."

He held up one hand to stop me from talking. "If you hustle anything like your father, we are getting ready to get paid. Oh, and for your information, your second guess was the right one."

"Huh?"

With the largest smile on his face, he whispered, "I'm the cheapest game in town. I sold him a half ounce for four hundred."

I put my fist to my lips and squealed, "Damn." Funny how Dee was the only person in the family who'd gotten an education, but he'd still wound up peddling dope like the rest of the hood. I would have never guessed that one.

In His Footsteps

Being with my cousin made me flash back to the days of living with my father. I could never forget my father's best friend Fat Daddy, AKA Fats. His name did not disappoint, because he was fat as hell. I used to feel so sorry for the young petite working girls at my dad's house when they'd been paid to sleep with his big ass. Not only was he fat, but he was about six feet tall. For some reason he believed that because he was light-skinned and had a lot of money, it compensated for his physique, but it didn't. The girls hated when he was there. One girl used to say it was the nastiest-looking ones who wanted you to do the freakiest shit to them.

Fats was never alone. He always took care of business with his two sons by his side. Rick and Danny were tall, light-skinned, but slender. I always wondered if they were his biological sons, because neither one of them was fat like him. The one thing my father loved was that Fats and his sons were in the drug game together. Almost like a mafia family. Even though I was only fifteen, my father had never hidden anything from me. I'd watch the four of them break down tens of thousands of dollars' worth of drugs right in front of me.

One time, Danny commented on how attentive I was to the process. "You look like you ready to come in with us."

Before I could answer, my father responded, "He'll let us know when he's ready."

That was the first time I realized that my father had aspirations for me to join him in the drug game, just like Fats and his boys. It wasn't an idea completely lost on me. After all, my father lived a pretty good life and hardly ever had to leave the house. That seemed a whole lot better than going to work every day.

Crack in the Foundation

My father had always been a cocaine dealer, but it seemed like the game was changing. Crack was the new thing. I didn't understand how cocaine was basically obsolete, yet crack was cocaine heated with baking soda and water. Once the combination came together, it made the cocaine hard like peanut brittle. Once the mixture was dry, you broke it up and sold it. However, there was something different about this stuff. It totally took over my mom and so many others. The people who came to my dad's house to buy it looked rough. All the new girls in the house were on it, and they looked rough too. It seemed like people had to have this stuff more than cocaine, even though it was basically the same thing.

Crack totally took over. In just a short period of time, I watched the world as I knew it crumble before my very eyes. My father's good friend Fats got murdered in a drug deal. Watching my dad mourn his friend made me hate crack even more. I was stunned when I looked over and saw my father crying as I sat beside him at Fats's funeral. I'd never seen my father cry before. As he tried to choke back the tears, I could hear him slowly whisper, "How could this happen?" I wasn't sure if he was crying for the good friend he'd lost, or because he'd lost his financial partner in crime.

There was one thing neither of us knew at the time. Things were about to get a whole lot worse, and in just three short months, my father was going to be murdered just like his best friend.

WOW, No Goodbye?

"Mississippi?" I grasped the top of my head. "Grandma, how can I be gone two days and you're telling me that my mother has moved to Mississippi to get clean and get herself together? No goodbye, no take care of yourself, no I love you, no good luck feeding yourself. What about me?" I shouted.

"At least she made sure you have a place to stay."

"Where is that?"

"Upstairs, where you were staying before. Rent is three hundred, and your Social Security check is three twenty-four. You gonna live upstairs, and that's that."

Before I could protest, Dee grabbed me and whispered, "Everything's cool. I got it all worked out."

"Dee, you knew about this?"

"Yeah, I worked it all out. Your mother is gone, and you got the place to yourself. This is your hood, right?"

"Yeah but—"

"But nothing. If you gonna sell dope, you gotta be in your hood, not living with me."

"Oh," I said and smiled.

"One more thing. Your mother signed custody of you over to me, so I can make decisions as your guardian."

My eyes widened to their fullest capacity. "What? When? How?"

It really had my jaws tight that my mother had just left. Signed over custody of me like it was nothing. My value felt less than a wet food stamp, but I had bigger problems. I'd lied and told my cousin that I'd sold dope with my father, but that had been pure bullshit. Just because I'd seen Pops sell drugs didn't mean I knew how to sell them.

Dee gave me a half ounce, but all I could do was stare at it. Where was I going to put it? Where was I going to sell it? *Damn, man, it looks like chipped-off pieces of soap.* I was totally confused and totally screwed. Then a lightbulb went off in my head. There were some guys who sold drugs right behind Moses Elementary School. Could I really be considering selling drugs behind the very school where I'd attended second and third grade? I'd had the leading role in the school play there, and now I was returning in my biggest role yet…acting like a drug dealer.

When I got to the school, I rounded the back end of the building where I saw three guys standing against the store on the corner. My heart was in my throat, but this was the only place I felt like I wouldn't get killed. Those guys watched me grow up, but they didn't know how far I'd grown. I just needed information on how to be a drug dealer, but I couldn't ask my cousin, because I was supposed to know already. These guys had the information I needed, so I had to get it out of them. I was going for it.

"What's up, fellas?"

"What's up, lil' Dave?"

"What's up! Why y'all out here looking all ugly?"

They all burst out laughing before one of the guys blurted out, "What yo lil' ass doing out here this late?"

"Man, I was asleep, and I just got the urge to see some ugly niggas and I knew y'all wouldn't let me down!"

They all exploded with laughter.

"Something just came over me while I was in the bed. A bright light said, I know where some ugly niggas hang out all the time."

Laughing hysterically, another guy said, "Fuck you, lil' bastard."

Thank you, Lord, for making me funny today. My nerves had me shaking so badly that I was about to pass out, but jokes got me in the door every time. "Hey, Big Dom, if somebody came around here with twenty dollars, how much crack would you give them?"

He was shocked and saddened by my statement. "Naw, little bro, I'm not gonna sell you no dope. You gonna have to get the hell outta here now."

The other guys overheard and began walking toward us to join the scolding.

Holy shit! Think. "Naw, fellas, it ain't like that. Look, I ain't gonna bullshit you. I got some dope to sell. Can you let me make a twenty-dollar sale so I can run in the store and buy me some Snickers bars, Cool Ranch Doritos, and a forty-ounce of St. Ides?"

They all burst out laughing.

"Just show me what I should give them." I opened my hand to expose a small amount of crack.

Big Dom grabbed it out of my hand and analyzed it. "It's about fifty dollars' worth." Stabbing his nail into it, he broke it into thirds. "Here, now you got two twenty-pieces and one ten-piece."

"Somebody gonna give me fifty bucks for these little pieces? Oh my God!" Before he could say anything, I jetted off, running home. My cousin had given me so much of the shit that I had to break it up to see what it amounted to.

I ran into my grandmother's house and sped up the stairs to my room. I reached under my bed and grabbed the bag. I took a plate and sat at the kitchen table with my heart racing. Once I

World's youngest drug dealer

emptied the crack onto the plate, I realized I had a problem. I didn't have any fingernails to break up the crack. I needed something sharp. *I know, I'll use a knife.* I plunged the knife into the crack, and it began to separate before my eyes. I had fifty twenty-pieces and twenty ten-pieces. *How much is that?* Grabbing my school calculator, I punched in the numbers. I couldn't believe it. It was over $1,200, and I only owed my cousin $400. This was the best feeling I'd ever felt in the world.

"Ouch," I squealed as I felt a pain in my crotch area. I stood up quickly, but didn't believe it! I'd just found out I was going to make $800 and my dick had gotten hard! I couldn't wait to tell somebody that shit.

Shop Relocated

It was almost ten thirty at night; I had a lot of drugs, but I still hadn't made my first drug deal. I decided to go back up to the block. I meant business this time. Big Dom had told me what to sell for twenty bucks, but I'd made my rocks bigger than his. I needed this money, and I was coming for it. I rounded the corner, nervous and excited at the same time, only to realize everybody was gone. *Where the hell is everyone?* What kind of drug operation had a curfew? Just as I began to get scared standing there by myself, I saw Big Dom walking back up in the distance.

"Where you go, little nigga? It's been some money coming through, but everybody out of dope."

"Damn, I got plenty. Where the hell the money go?"

Before I could get the words out, Dom said, "There goes some now."

A gold Cutlass slowly pulled to the curb, and a thin, scary-looking man asked Big Dom, "Y'all back on yet?"

"Yeah, we on. My lil' nigga got you right here."

Everything in my mind was trying to walk toward the car, but my body wasn't moving. From about twenty feet away, I shouted, "What you need?" I was hoping he wouldn't see my nervousness and just pull away, but he really wanted what I had. I represented his high. Those small crumbs represented everything to him, so he wasn't leaving without them.

"I got fifty."

Damn, fifty? I felt extreme excitement. As I walked the twenty feet over to the rattling car, it seemed like a mile. One foot in front of the other; I couldn't help but think that this was the very activity that had gotten my dad killed. Arriving at the car window, I reached forward and dropped three stones in his hand. Far more than he'd paid for, but I wanted him to be happy and not kill me.

"Daaaamn, young blood. All this for fifty?"

"Yeah, this time, but only if you come back and see me." I borrowed that line from my father when he'd given someone a good deal.

The crackhead sped off like a bat outta hell.

"Why the hell he speed off so fast, Big Dom?"

He laughed. "That's because he's in a hurry to go smoke that shit."

I raised my eyebrows. "Damn!"

Elle B. Six

•••

Unbelievable! Two hundred and thirty dollars my first night. I knew it was $230 because I counted it fifty-two times. I'd never held this much cash before. That was what it was about right there. My Social Security check was $324 per month, and I'd almost made that in three hours. I had my own house. *Hell, I'm a bachelor at fifteen. I inherited this hustle from my father. He lives through me, and I have to do what I got to do to survive!*

The next day I was still riding the high from the night before. I grabbed some dope to head back over to the block. "What's up, Big Dom?"

Instead of answering, he gave me a shady, irritated look as a response.

"What's up? Everything good, big bro?"

"Naw, little nigga, you can't hustle up here no mo."

Puzzled, I questioned, "What? Why?"

"Because this is our block, and we the only people getting money up here. Yo' lil' ass gon' have to go somewhere else!"

"Damn, I thought you was teaching me the ropes?"

While we were talking, the ugly guy in the gold Cutlass pulled up. "Shorty, where you been? I been looking for you all day." Big Dom walked to the car in an attempt to serve him, but the customer would have none of it. "I came for lil' man."

Angrily, Dom told him, "Lil man don't work here no mo."

Feeling cocky, I yelled out, "Yeah, I'm working at the Jamison playground from now on. Come see me."

Walking back home, my eyes began to well with tears. *That's not fair. Why should I have to leave because customers like my stuff better?* I was having an adolescent tantrum about a very grown-up game of life or death. If I was going to make a name for myself, I needed to start my own block. *Jamison Park, here I come.*

Sleeping in the Jungle

Jamison Park-Harvard Saga begins

I knew I could get that new block started, because Dee had the best dope in town and the lowest prices. Wherever the good dope was, the dope fiends would come. Selling those crumbs was the easiest thing in the world. People came with money and you just gave them a crumb. Dee was becoming my father reincarnated. Although I was pissed that my mother had just given me away, I was happy to be with him. He reminded me so much of my dad. No nonsense. A hustler to his heart but also a caring male figure. He made sure I had food in the house, nice clothes, and plenty of money. *How could I be so lucky?*

Even Grandma was turning around. My cousin didn't hide what we were doing from her, although I told him we should. She liked the money we were making, and to my astonishment, she wanted to get in on it. My cousin was contemplating taking a trip up to New York City to buy drugs. This trip would cut out the local dealers and make our drug prices even cheaper. My grandmother took out a second mortgage on her home to help finance part of the deal. *Oh my God, am I about to be selling dope for my disabled grandmother?* I thought. That would take family dysfunction to a whole new level!

The school year was over, and summer was about to be in full swing. I walked out of the house on an average summer night about to head to the block, and I saw Dee standing behind his car with the trunk open.

"What's up, Dee? When are you heading out?"

"I'm leaving Friday, but I don't want to hear about you talking to nobody about this."

Nonchalantly I turned my head. "Uh-huh…yeah." Out of nowhere, I felt my entire rib cage shake. BOOM! I leaned forward because the pain was too great to stand upright. "Damn, cuz, why did you hit me?"

He looked at me through hollow eyes. "Talk to nobody, you hear me?" He jumped in his car and pulled off. *Damn, he didn't have to hit me.* But I knew silence was the key to success in the game. I'd never seen this side of my cousin, but I knew he was nervous. We had a lot riding on this. Like my father used to say, "Whatever it takes!"

Run, Nigga, Run

appy Birthday! In true hustler's fashion, I was ringing in my sixteenth birthday in a crack house. I had this house pumping most of the summer, and the traffic was starting to get outrageous. Crackhead Sam had a house on the opposite end of the playground where I hustled. It was a funky-looking single-family house that was dingy white with green trim. The walls were yellow from all the smoking that went on, and there was very little furniture. His house doubled as a place to sell dope and chill after hours. However, there was no dope being sold tonight; I was partying!

Three fifths of Mad Dog 20/20, three girls, and a mean-ass sack of weed. My night was set to go! I'd never even had a ménage à trois before, so I was super excited to kick my first one off with a foursome. These were just local neighborhood girls, and their only ambition in life was to date drug dealers. They were in their late teens. They weren't that attractive, but they weren't that ugly either. In fact, the more I drank, the prettier they were getting. The weed was for the girls, because I didn't smoke, but the drink was for us all. After I filled my cup up for the third time, I started to feel light-headed. I think I got a contact high off the weed smoke, too. The girls began sucking each other's pussies, but I was too drunk to do anything except watch with a stupid-ass look on my face.

I felt Crackhead Sam pushing on my shoulder. "Wake up! It's morning. You have to go before my wife gets home."

Groggy, I asked, "What, it's morning? Where did the girls go?"

"They left after you fell asleep."

"OH, NO! My first ménage à trois, and I fell asleep! On my birthday? Why the hell didn't anybody wake me up?"

"Man, they tried to wake you up over and over. Your ass was passed out."

Before he could finish his account of the night, I got a sinking feeling in my chest. It was morning, and I wasn't allowed to stay out all night. I dashed out of the house and ran up Miles Avenue toward my grandmother's house. I knew my cousin was due to return today, and I was hopeful I could slip into the house without anyone noticing.

"Damn." My cousin's car was in the driveway. *Man, this dude is about to be pissed off! I may as well just walk in and face the music. Shit, he knows yesterday was my birthday. I'm just going to tell him I went hard last night. Dee was sixteen before. He is just going to have to understand.*

As soon as I opened the door, my cousin picked me up in the air by my clothes and slammed me on my back.

"Dee, what the hell you doing?"

"Oh, you think you grown, muthafucka?" He kicked me in the chest and completely knocked the wind out of me. It felt like my insides were on fire.

"Wait, cuz, I was drunk and fell asleep."

Unmoved by my explanation, he delivered a devastating blow to my midsection and threw me from one end of the room to the other. His strength was incredible, and his rage was like nothing I'd ever seen. Unable to catch my breath from the hit, I watched in horror as he walked toward me again. My eyes started to fill with tears, and he proceeded to reach down for what I thought was another blow, but instead, he offered me assistance.

He lifted me off the floor onto the couch. "Don't cry, cuz. I'm sorry. I just want the best for you because I love you."

I was glad my tears somehow had reached his soft side, because I didn't know how I was going to get him to stop. My dad never hit me, but this crazy guy was all I had! "I'm sorry too, cuz, but I was trying to tell you that I never intended to stay out all night. It was truly a mistake. I consumed more alcohol than I normally drink because it was my birthday and passed out, nothing more." Although I'd stemmed the tide of violence with a few tears, I was beginning to have an uneasy feeling about my new guardian.

The next day I woke up and started to head out the back door, and I saw my grandmother sitting in her kitchen. "Good morning, Grandma."

She turned and looked straight through me. "What's so good about it?"

"What's wrong?"

"That nigga didn't tell you?"

"What nigga? Tell me what?"

"Your cousin went up there to New York with all of our money and got robbed."

My eyes widened with shock. "No way, really?" Damn, he'd gotten robbed and my dumb ass had stayed out all night the day he'd gotten back. I felt so bad! No wonder he'd been so upset. "Don't worry about it. I'll help him get things back on track. We'll get your money back for the house, I promise."

When Dee arrived at the house later that day, I couldn't wait to console him. "Damn, Grandma told me what happened. What are you going to do?"

For the first time, I saw Dee becoming emotional. As the tears streamed down his face, he screamed, "I don't know what the fuck I'm gonna do! I lost all my money, Grandma's money, and two of my partners' money." He screamed in pure pain and fury. "These Spanish muthafuckas had me hemmed up. I had to give them the money or they were gonna kill me." Dee continued to cry but calmed his tone. "I just had a baby boy. I couldn't die up there over no money. Fuck!"

I felt so powerless because I was unable to help my cousin while he was going through this tough time. I could see the pain reeling through his heart as he contemplated how he was going to put things back together. My first instinct was self-preservation. I couldn't let this man fall apart. Without him, where did that leave me? *How can I bring him back from his sense of hopelessness?* Before I finished that thought, I knew what I needed to do. I looked my cousin dead in his eyes and said, "Yeah, well, I don't feel sorry for yo ass! While you were getting yo dumb ass robbed, I fell asleep on three girls sucking each other's pussies."

He burst out laughing, his face still drenched with tears.

"What about my sense of loss? I fell asleep on three girls, didn't get so much as a finger in the pussy, and on top of that, you whooped my ass."

"You crazy as hell, cuz."

"Crazy? Naw, yo ass is crazy. You in here crying over some punk-ass money. We can always make more money. I can't ever get my sweet sixteen back. I don't have time to be sitting around looking sad. Man, drop me the fuck off on the block."

We jumped in his car, and three jokes later we were already talking game plan.

"I can sell all the dope you get, cuz. Let's use my youth to get the money back."

"Dave, not only do I not have any dope, I only have a thousand dollars to my name."

Sleeping in the Jungle

"It's cool, you got a thousand bucks. I know a guy on the other side of town who's been trying to front me some dope for a while. I got us covered!"

• • •

I did have us covered. I made one phone call to my man DJ from Superior Avenue, and we were about to be back in the game. I asked DJ to front me an eighth of a key, and we had a thousand dollars down on it. I finally saw a sense of hope coming from Dee. He'd never thought the person to rescue him from his ordeal would be me! It was my sixteen-year-old ass who made the local connections. Dee and I were becoming as close as ever. Kind of like the father-and-son team I could've had with my real father.

"Here he come now."

"What's up, DJ? I told you I was going to hit you up one day."

DJ smiled. "It's about time you decided to get on a real team. This is four and a half ounces, youngster. The price is twenty-five hundred, so imma take this grand and you owe me fifteen hundred."

"No problem! Can I get about a week to finish?"

Surprised and delighted at the short time period I needed to sell the dope, he quickly agreed.

"Okay, cool," I replied as I exited the car.

"Here you go, cuz. We got a week to dump this." I couldn't recall ever seeing my cousin this happy. I knew my cousin could sell that dope in less than an hour and flip the money many times over by the next week. We were back in the game big time. All I had to do was let him work his magic, and we'd be golden. Watching my cousin pull off on his journey to put our family back on track was the most fulfilling moment I'd had in a long time. I felt a sense of worth again. I felt like I belonged again. As I slid into bed that night, I knew everything was going to be okay.

"David, wake up."

Out of a dead sleep I looked up and saw Dee. "What's up?"

"How the fuck do you know this DJ nigga?"

"I'm confused. You mean DJ who just fronted us the dope?"

"You mean the muthafucka who fronted us the fake dope?"

"What? Fake? What you mean?"

Without hesitation, he swung his hand and slapped me so hard that it felt like my cheek was on fire. "That was the last thousand dollars I had in this world. Show me where this muthafucka live." Before I could answer, he screamed again, "Where the fuck does he live?"

I never knew that telling Dee where DJ lived meant we'd go there that night. As I watched my cousin load up guns in the kitchen, I couldn't help wishing I could just grab one of them and kill myself right then. "What's the plan?" I asked my cousin and two of his henchmen, Head and Baby. I knew Head and Baby weren't going to answer because they looked big, slow, and dumb. Head didn't even have all his front teeth.

Dee directed pure hatred and contempt toward me. "You gon' take yo' lil' ass up to the door and knock. When the door opens, we going in to get my fuckin' money back."

I thought that was the dumbest plan I'd ever heard. I'd be right in the line of fire between both of them if this thing went south, but I knew not to say a word.

I'm smarter than these three jerks put together, but it doesn't take a rocket scientist to know this is going to turn out bad. Lord, if you're real, I really need your help on this one!

We loaded up and headed off in the car.

"Which house is it?"

"Right over there," I instructed as my heart began to beat out of my chest.

"Are you ready?" they asked simultaneously.

They parked with the lights off. "What's the plan again?" I repeated as if I didn't know their stupid-ass idea.

Sleeping in the Jungle

"Don't bitch out, muthafucka. You want to play the big-boy game, now it's time to do big-boy shit."

Click. Click. Click. All three men exited. *Choom. Choom. Choom.* All three doors closed, but I was still sitting in the car, frozen stiff.

Dee opened my door and attempted to put me at ease. "Don't be scared. Just knock on the door and get the fuck out the way."

I slid out of the back seat and stood on a neighboring tree lawn. *Oh my God.* My stomach began to lurch into dry heaves, but I was too scared to throw up. *I'm losing my breath! I gotta think. I gotta do something. I gotta do something, but what? Help me, Jesus. I can't do it. Please think.* "Uh, wait guys, I gotta use the bathroom."

"Quit stalling, goddamn it. We doing this shit right now!"

"Look, Dee, man, I'm down with this shit. Just let me go on the side of one of these neighbor's houses before I piss on myself. I'm scared as hell!"

"Okay, hurry up, goddammit."

I reached the bushes on the side of an unknown house, and I pulled out my penis and aimed at the bushes. I really didn't have to pee, but I needed a few more seconds to think. I couldn't think of one joke to tell that could get me out of this situation. *Please, Eddie Murphy, Red Foxx, somebody send me a joke so that I can fix this.* I aimed at the bushes for just a few more seconds, but not a single joke came to mind from any of the great comedians of the world. As I carefully tucked my manhood back in my pants and prepared to embrace my fate, I felt a bolt of courage from deep in my soul that quieted my fear. All of a sudden, I heard a booming voice inside of my head that said, "RUN, NIGGA, RUN."

No Time for Tears

I took off like a bat out of hell. I jumped each fence like I was in the

Olympics. Three streets later, I was out of breath, but this was no time to be tired. I had to keep going. *Oh, shit, headlights!* The shine from the lights shot through my body like a bullet, and my eyes opened wider than they ever had before. I took off running again. Swoosh, swoosh, as I dashed through the yards. "Can't keep running," I whispered through extreme exhaustion with hands on both knees. I looked around the yard I was standing in and spotted a van. I rolled up under it and lay as still as possible.

What the hell are you going to do now, asshole? As I stared straight up at the van's oily exhaust pipe, I began to tear up. *I'll lie here all night if I have to. At least I'm safe. I'm not killing anybody! Those fools are crazy! Where the hell am I going to go? How will I live? My cousin is my guardian, and as far as I know, he could be looking to hurt me for what I just did. I had to run. I can't go to my grandma's; I can't go anywhere. There's one thing for sure. I can't go back with Dee. I'm supposed to start eleventh grade in a couple of days and I'm in dire straits. I'll go to school by day and hustle at night until I get enough money to get my own place. I have to try and make it on my own until I'm eighteen. I'm a hustler; I know I can do it. Just one problem. I only have three hundred bucks to my name. I've got a long way to go.*

After a few hours of lying under the van, I was ready to take my chances that the coast was clear. I walked out of the yard and felt like my cousin was going to jump out of every bush and grab me. I was cutting down side streets and avoiding every set of headlights until I got back to the hood. Finally arriving at Crackhead Sam's house, I felt so blessed to be alive.

"What's up, Sam? What's up, my brother?" I said to a stranger sitting on the couch across from Sam.

"What's up?" they both replied in cadence.

"Y'all ain't gonna believe what happened to me. Before I tell you this story, Sam, I need you to call somebody up so I can buy some dope."

"How much?"

"Tell them I want a dub for three hundred." While Sam was ordering the dope, an overwhelming feeling of exhaustion came over me. The short, light-skinned stranger rose to his feet so that I could stretch out on the couch. "Sam, can I crash here for a few days?"

Of course, the answer was yes if I had some dope. Another good situation. Keep some dope, keep a place to stay. No problem!

•••

The first day of school was a complete blast. It was nice seeing my classmates back from summer break. Everyone was so concerned about me because the last thing they remembered from the end of last school year was my dad's murder. They could see that I was living a rough lifestyle, but my ego made me believe I was looking good. I flashed money and talked big, but I looked and smelled like I came to school from a crack house. No matter what happened in my life, I had to go to school. My dad always told me that the only way we could get out of this life was by earning an education. I promised him I'd finish high school, and nothing would keep me from it.

Living with Crackhead Sam was sweet. I came and went as I pleased as long as I kept him supplied with drugs. My drug sales over the next few days turned my $300 into $1,000. "Sam, call me up a dub for a thousand bucks," I said cockily to Sam and the light-skinned stranger from the other night. "Let me know when the dope gets here, and I'm going to take me a quick after-school nap."

"Okay, cool. I got you. I'm about to run to the store. Do you want something?"

"Naw, I'm good." I let out a yawn. As the door closed, I instantly began to enjoy the silence.

Wham.

I could only open one eye after the shock, but I could feel that I'd been hit in the head with something. "Uh-uh, what the fuck?"

Wham!

"Aaah, shit. Help!"

"Shut up, lil' nigga," a voice demanded.

As my eyes cleared, I saw it was the stranger. "Ah man, what the hell you hit me with? Why the fuck did you hit me?"

The stranger lifted the bottle again. It was dripping with blood from the wound on my head. "Give me yo money, you lil' bitch, or I'm gon' bash yo' head in."

"Wait, man, you don't understand!"

Wham!

The final blow landed, and I relented. I gave him all the money I had in the world, and he dashed out the door. *What the fuck just happened?*

I treated my wounds in Sam's bathroom and tried to come to terms with what had happened.

Sam walked into the house, and his eyes widened with shock at my condition. "What happened, Lil Dave?"

"That nigga you had in here busted my head and robbed me, that's what happened!"

"What?"

"Yeah. Conveniently after you went to the store, he robs me." My sarcasm implied that he might have been in on it with the stranger, and he instantly withdrew his concern for my wound.

"Hold on, muthafucka. You trying to say I had something to do with this shit?" Before I could make any effort to soften my accusations, he cut me off. "You got me fucked up, lil' nigga. You got to get the fuck out of my house talking that shit."

With extreme remorse, I tried to talk him down, because I had no-

Sleeping in the Jungle

where else to go. Hearing none of it, he promptly walked me out the door and slammed it.

Damn, how could this much bad shit happen to me in this short-ass period of time? Not only did I get robbed for every dime I have in the world, but now I have nowhere to go.

My friend Aaron lived a couple of streets away. He slept in the basement by himself and sometimes he'd sneak me in to play video games, but that night I needed something different.

Tink, tink, tink. I lightly rapped on the basement glass-block facing the driveway. I hoped he was in the basement or I was screwed. I rejoiced as the glass-block window opened.

"Who is it?" he whispered.

"It's Dave."

"Oh, what's up, Dave? What's going on?"

"Yo, Aaron man, let me in right quick, bro. I'm in trouble!"

I'd known Aaron since we were in preschool. I spilled my heart out, and he felt every ounce of my pain. He ran upstairs and grabbed me something to eat.

"Thanks, bro." I devoured the leftovers.

Aaron expressed extreme sorrow for my situation. "You can hide out here for a while. Don't worry, I got you."

Thank God! Finally, someone was concerned about me. I hid out at Aaron's for the next week. No one had a clue where the hell I was. He let me wear some of his clothes to school, and he didn't mind because we went to different schools. It was a good situation. Aaron kept me fed and we played video games all night. When his grandparents left for work, I'd run up and shower. I was grateful to get a break from my chaotic life.

As I watched Aaron sleep on his single box-spring mattress in a basement that he shared only with the washing machine and dryer, I couldn't help but think about how lucky he was. I began falling asleep on the floor beside him.

Just as I fell asleep, I overheard a faint voice in the distance. "Aaron, Aaron. What the hell is this drug boy doing in my house?"

Oh shit. It's Aaron's grandfather!

"Get up, boy, and get out of my house," he said in his Southern-accented voice.

"I'm so sorry, sir. I just came over to play video games and fell asleep."

"I don't give a damn what you were doing. Don't bring yo ass back over here trying to corrupt my grandson."

Wow, why does he think I'm trying to corrupt his grandson? I'd never do anything to negatively influence Aaron. We've been friends since elementary school. When I stood on street corners selling drugs, I guess I never thought about who would judge me for it.

As I moved toward the steps, I turned to look at Aaron just as his grandfather laid into him with his leather belt. Damn, I'd just got my friend an ass-whooping—but worse than that, I was officially back on the streets again. Just as my eyes were beginning to well with tears, I caught myself. This was no time for crying; this was big-boy time for real. This was real life. This was the final curtain call. Life or death. I chose life, but would death choose me?

The Jungle Gym
CLEVELAND, OHIO
FALL 1992

It was 8:55. Only five minutes left before the store closed and I wouldn't be able to get warm for the rest of the night. There had to be at least one more door I could knock on. One more couch, one more basement, one more crack house? Nothing! My welcome was worn out. How could I be homeless at sixteen?

The minute hand ticked to 8:58. Mike, the store's owner, blurted out in his Middle Eastern accent, "Time to go, buddy. Closing in two minutes."

Thinking on my toes, I hurried over to the liquor section to grab a fifth of Thunderbird, two packs of Kool-Aid, and four bags of potato chips.

When I approached the counter, I knew he could see the pain glaring through my young eyes. "No charge, buddy. Pay me next time."

I was standing in front of the recently closed store on the corner of East 138th and Harvard with eleven dollars left in my pocket and nowhere to go. It was forty degrees outside and the wind snatched the tears from my eyes like a waterfall. Who cries for the sixteen-year-old boy who'd had two parents and a stable home just one year ago?

The closest thing I felt to love were the three layers of clothes that hugged my small frame. *If I could just escape this wind… If I could block these piercing wind gusts, I may survive the night.*

The only protection I saw from the wind was a small enclosure placed at the top of a sliding board in the middle of the Jamison playground. The enclosure atop the sliding board that we nicknamed the Jungle Gym was a three-foot-by-three-foot structure shaped like a dollhouse. It would perfectly conceal my 120-pound frame.

What if somebody sees me climbing in? I'd rather die in the waters of Lake Erie before I live with the embarrassment of someone seeing me sleeping in the playground. I walked around for nearly an hour, making sure the coast was clear.

"It's now or never."

I climbed up the sliding board and eased into the small shelter. Although I was overcome by the biggest sense of relief, it was immediately shattered by the nightmare that was my reality.

Why is no one looking for me? I'm homeless in a world I know nothing about. "Somebody please help me? Please?" I screamed as my tears slowly began to flow.

● ● ●

If the Lord had a plan for my life, it wasn't going to be fulfilled crying in this Jungle Gym. *Lord, I thank you for not allowing me to smell like this anymore. I thank you that one day, people won't make fun of me anymore. I thank you that I won't ever be hungry like this again. I thank you for saving me from having to sleep in this Jungle Gym ever again. I thank you that one day I'm going to be sitting in my mansion and thinking about this moment and laughing at how far I've come. First thing's first though, Lord. Can you please just keep me warm tonight? Please don't let me die like this! In your son Jesus Christ's name, Amen.*

Sleeping in the Jungle

As the sun came up, I carefully slid out of the Jungle Gym to head to school. I still had a half a bottle of Thunderbird and there was no way I was leaving it. I tucked it in my coat, and two bus tickets later I was walking up to the school. I hid my bottle on the side of the school steps before entering the building and prayed nobody found it before I left to go home.

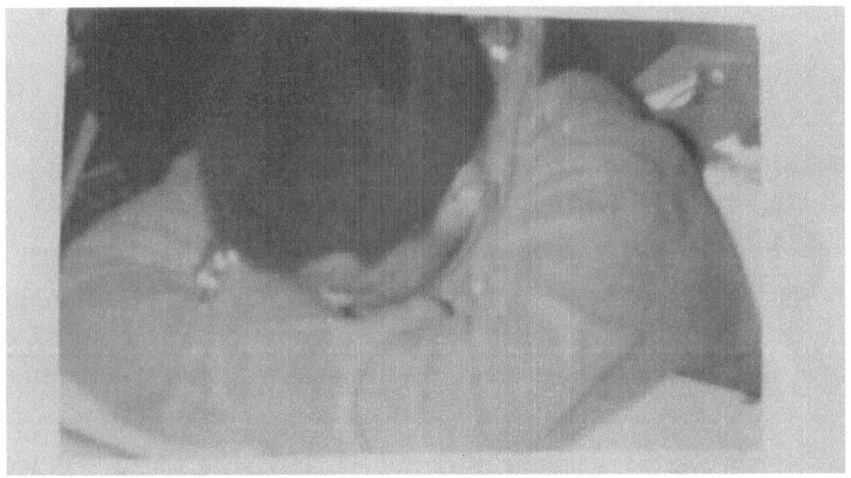

Got my best sleep on a school desk

School represented two things: heat and sleep. I got some of the best sleep in my life on the top of those hard-top desks. I wore the same clothes every day. I hadn't had a shower since forever. I had to smell like straight liquor, but none of my teachers ever bothered me because they were happy that I was still showing up.

The news of my father's murder and my family situation was widespread throughout the school among both faculty and students. There were many people rooting for me that I didn't even know about. Later the same day at school, I caught wind of a plot that my fellow classmates hatched without my knowledge. Sarah and Jonesy had been completing my class assignments and turning them in to the teachers so I could pass. Sarah was a quiet girl I'd been going to school with since seventh grade. She was Caucasian with long red hair. Jonesy was the opposite of quiet. He was crazier than me and had always been my friend. He brought me in clothes and food because he knew all the things I was going through. He was a tall black kid with a big belly.

"Why are you guys doing all of my work and turning it in for me?"

Jonesy's response was simple. "Because we love you. If you promise to keep coming, we promise to keep doing the work."

I'd never cried so much in my life. "This is really the nicest thing anybody's ever done for me. I love y'all too, and I promise I'll never drop out."

My father had a seventh-grade education, and my mother only made it to tenth grade. I always thought about the promise that I made my dad, so the least I could do was keep showing up.

I walked into math class to get my last hour of sleep before I hit the streets. I heard the teacher ask, "What are two numbers that when multiplied together equal negative eighteen but when added together equal seven?"

Before I sat down, I answered, "Nine and negative two."

Everybody, including the teacher, looked at me with amazement. "How in the world do you understand algebra and you don't do anything in my class but sleep?"

"That's not algebra. That question is multiplication and addition. I saw you do that yesterday before I went to sleep, so I don't need to see you do it again. Now please don't ask me any more questions because I'm tired." Everybody laughed, and I laid my head down on the desk.

SLEEPING IN THE JUNGLE

BAD TO WORSE

I left school that day with a new vigor. My classmates would never know how they inspired me when I was at my lowest point. I vowed that last night was the final night I was sleeping in that Jungle Gym. I got off the bus at 138th and Harvard. I only had eleven dollars and I needed to try to double it. As soon as I got to the block, I saw the coolest white Cadillac rolling up with a red ragtop and 100-spoke Daytons. As the window rolled down, I saw it was one of the OGs from the hood named Black.

"What's up, Black?"

"What the fuck you doin' up here, lil'-ass nigga? I know you don't call yourself hustling now?"

I laughed. "The hell I ain't. In fact, I'm trying to get a dub for these ten dollars."

"Hahaha—ten dollars, auuuuuuuurghh hurrr." This guy had the most annoying laugh in history. He was laughing at my ten dollars like it was nothing, but it was the last ten I had in the world. Just as I was about to say fuck you, he pulled out the biggest bag of crack I'd ever seen in my life. He broke me off some pieces and took my ten dollars. I looked in my hand with amazement. He'd given me about two hundred dollars' worth of dope.

I couldn't believe my luck. *If there's one thing I know for sure, I'm not sleeping in that Jungle Gym tonight.* I knew I couldn't hold that much dope on me, so I sold some and stashed the rest in the bushes. After I made a couple more sales, I returned to where I'd stashed the drugs, and they were gone.

Oh no, who stole my shit? Everybody on the block looked around, but nobody seemed to know. I had about forty dollars in cash and sixty dollars' worth of dope left. They'd stolen half of everything I had just as fast as I'd gotten it. *Damn, I hate scandalous muthafuckas. Please Lord, don't let me wind up back in that Jungle Gym.*

Just as my feelings of lowness returned, a sale came for some drugs. It was Crazy E from Garfield. Crazy E had the biggest eyeballs I'd ever seen. He was skinny as hell and you could tell that he smoked crack long before he asked you for some. His hands were always filthy like he was working on cars, and the first thing he wanted to do was touch you.

"What's up, E?"

"You got something for fifty?"

"Hell yeah." I jumped in the car with him and gave him the sixty dollars' worth of dope I had—for fifty dollars. While we were riding, I looked around the car and noticed it was destroyed. "Damn, Crazy E, why is your car all tore up?"

"This ain't my damn car. I stole this from across town and I got all I need off it so I'm about to go dump it."

"Naw, don't dump it. Let me have it."

"Naw, lil nigga. This car's hot, and if you get caught in it you going to jail."

"I can take care of myself, E. If I get caught, I don't know you."

Tired of the debate, he relented. "I'll tell you what. Drop me off and I don't give a damn what you do with it. You'd just better get rid of it in the next couple of days because the police are going to be looking for it."

● ● ●

To me, that stolen car represented a good night's rest. After I filled the tank up with gas, I slowly eased the modest sedan around the back of an abandoned house. I left the car idling behind the house with the heat blowing on me all night long. The best thing about Crazy E was that he was a notorious car thief. He agreed that every time he finished stripping a stolen car, I could use it to sleep in for a couple of nights before I dumped

Sleeping in the Jungle

it. It really was a good relationship; the only thing that sucked was that he lived in the city of Garfield, which was known for police harassment.

As I was driving into Garfield to get a different car, the police spotted how young I looked driving the new car. I was barely able to see over the dashboard, so I didn't notice they were following me. I led them straight to E's house. Just as I was opening the door, I heard, "FREEEEEZE. GET THE FUCK ON THE GROUND—NOW."

As the handcuffs were tightened around my wrists, the officer whispered in my ear, "You're under arrest, asshole."

The best thing about getting arrested as a minor was that you only needed a guardian to come and pick you up. The problem was, Dee was my guardian and there was no way in hell I was calling him. I racked my brain trying to think of an adult who would stand in as my guardian, and the only person I could come up with was Crackhead Sam. I was nervous about calling him, but I had no choice.

"Hello?"

"Hello, Sam. It's Dave. Please don't hang up. Look, man, I'm in jail and I don't have anybody to come get me. If you pretend to be my guardian, I will give you a hundred dollars' worth of dope."

The offer was too good to resist. He showed up within the hour, furious with me like a real parent. It was a Hollywood performance for sure as he slapped me on the back of the head and assured a lengthy punishment for my actions. After signing some paperwork, we were on our way. Pulling out of the police station, I couldn't control my happiness to be free. "Thanks, Sam. Man, I thought you were my dad for real."

Sam laughed. "Yeah, but I was nervous as hell. I just kept thinking they were gonna throw my black ass in jail too." Pulling up to his house, he finally asked, "Where do you need to go to get the hundred bucks' worth of shit?"

"Oh, you can have it whenever you're ready for it. All you have to do is call up the nigga who robbed me in your house and tell him to shoot it to you." I got out of the car and mouthed *blow me* before I shut the door.

The Pink Robe

"DAVID KING TO THE FRONT OFFICE, PLEASE. DAVID KING TO THE FRONT OFFICE," the school intercom announced.

Why the hell are they calling me over the intercom? This was new. *Whatever happened, I didn't do it, so I have nothing to worry about.* Unfazed, I walked into the front office, but in an instant, my heart sank. There was my cousin Dee!

The assistant principal, Dr. Almond, was in the office next to Dee. Dee was standing in the doorway with the look of an angered parent, but I knew his anger came from a different place. He stared at me with crossed arms and squinted eyes, and my heart felt like it quit beating. Although Dr. Almond was a six-foot-tall Caucasian man, I hardly noticed he was even there until he proclaimed, "Well, it seems you're a runaway, huh, Mr. King?"

My body was so riveted with terror that I couldn't even respond. Because Dee was my legal guardian and he'd reported me as a runaway, that technically made me a runaway.

"I understand that this is the last time we'll be seeing you. You're going to live with your mother in Mississippi. We wish you the best of luck, and I know things will work out for the best in your new environment."

As we walked out of the front office, I couldn't help but think I should've said something to the assistant principal. I should've tried to signal him with my eyes, but when things are happening in real time,

Sleeping in the Jungle

you don't know what to do. *My God, I'm in trouble.* Before I opened the car door, I needed to test where this guy's head was at. "Look, Dee, I know things got fucked up that night I ran, but I was so scared and—"

"Don't worry about that, cuz. I'm sorry! I never should have had you in that situation. I was mad about my money and I'm glad things didn't go down that night."

Relieved by the assurance that he wasn't bitter, I couldn't help but ask, "Where are we headed?"

"Oh, you're going to chill out at my house until your bus leaves to take you to Mississippi with your mother."

It took a few minutes to swallow the information. *I can't go to Mississippi. I can't tell him that I was arrested in a stolen car and that'll make it impossible for me to leave town, because I don't know how he'll react.* "I'm really not trying to go to Mississippi."

"Look, I can't be your guardian anymore because I got problems of my own. You're going down there with your mother, and that's that."

Man, how the hell am I going to get away from this dude? As soon as I get an opportunity to break away, I'm taking off.

By the time we pulled up to Dee's house, I was planning ways I could get away. Walking in, my eyes bulged with shock. The house was completely empty except for a couch and a TV!

"What's up, Dee? You moving?"

"Yeah, I'm moving and you gonna stay here until your bus leaves. I know you like to run away, so I'm gonna need you to strip out of your clothes."

"What? Strip?" I asked. I thought the request must have been a joke.

"Yeah, strip. Take off all yo muthafuckin' clothes so I know you won't run out this bitch. Unless you gonna run out naked."

Defiant, I sat on the couch and crossed my arms. "I ain't takin' off my clothes, bro."

Elle B. Six

Like clockwork, he threw a punch. Boom, right to my throat. I knew it was coming, so I leaned away and took some of the impact off the blow. He was so predictable, I instantly started crying because every time I started crying, he stopped hitting me and said he loved me. Tears were flowing; next thing you knew, he reached out to hug me. This guy was dumber than a box of rocks. I couldn't believe I ever looked up to him. I relented and took off my clothes just to get him out of my face.

"Look, cuz. I love you, but you goin' to Mississippi and I'm finished talking about it. I'll be back about eight o'clock." He snatched his keys out of his pocket and walked out the door with my clothes.

I sat in the empty house with no clothes on, but I was furious. I knew he was probably watching to see if I would try to leave. I searched the house for something to put on. I looked in every room, but the place was completely empty. Nothing in the closets, no appliances, no bedroom sets, and no clothes anywhere. I kept peering out the window to see if I saw him anywhere watching. *Something about this doesn't feel right. Why would he leave me in an empty house naked? Dee could have easily kept me with him until the bus leaves.*

The more I searched around this house, the more I realized it looked like the perfect place to kill somebody. *What if there is no bus ticket? What if he's coming after eight because it'll be dark? I gotta take my chances and run up outta here, but it's broad daylight. What the hell should I do? This guy is my cousin; he wouldn't really kill me, would he? I tell you one thing, I can't sit around and figure it out.* Overwhelmed with fear, I cursed God! "God, where the hell are You? Look at this!" I screamed in anger. With tears rolling down my face, I began to reflect on the last six months. "How can You save me just to leave me like this?"

Exhausted from anger and fear, I fell asleep. Upon waking, I checked the clock; it was five thirty. More than four hours had passed. *He can't still be watching. It's now or never. I have to make a run for it, but I don't want to run out of the house naked.* Out of desperation, I searched the house one more time. There had to be something there I could cover myself with. I opened the closet right next to the couch I was sleeping on, and to my amazement there was a bright pink bathrobe. I slammed the door shut because I knew that I'd searched that closet three different times earlier. It had to be a trick. Dee must be in the house.

Gripped with fear, I walked around the rest of the house, checking for where he could be hiding. From top to bottom, there was no one there. I returned to the couch and asked myself, *If someone put the robe there, wouldn't you hear them open the closet right next to you? Why would Dee plant clothes for me to run in the first place?* I knew the robe hadn't been there before, but I couldn't afford to sit there and contemplate where it came from. *Running down the street in a pink robe would be embarrassing, but it's not as embarrassing as running down the street naked. I'm outta here!*

I ran with the pink robe on, and my heart was about to pump out of my chest. Every car I saw looked like Dee's. Trembling with fear, I ran across Euclid Avenue to the East Cleveland Cleaners. I entered the establishment, ran behind the counter, and ducked beside the Chinese owner's leg. "Please, sir, I'm in trouble. Can I use your phone?"

"What's wrong?"

"Sir, I've been kidnapped, and I just need to make a phone call."

Unsure if he should just call the police because of the way I was hiding behind his counter, he politely offered me his business phone.

The most amazing thing in the world was that my number one priority was to get to a phone, but I didn't know who the heck I was about to call. I couldn't call the police, because they might send me back to Dee. I couldn't call Crackhead Sam because I'd screwed him out of his last $100.

A revelation hit me while I was staring at the phone. My father had a sister who lived in East Cleveland. I had not seen her since the funeral.

As a kid, I always made a joke about how easy her number was to remember. It was 555-5553, the same number twice with a 3 on the end. When I dialed, all I could think was, *I sure hope this is still the number.*

"Hello?"

"Uh, hello, Auntie?"

"Yes baby, is this David? What a pleasant surprise!"

"Uh, Auntie, I was wondering if you could come pick me up."

"Yeah, what's wrong, baby? Where are you?"

By now I was in tears. The sound of her voice made me so anxious. I almost felt as if I could get out of this alive if she could just hear my desperation. "I'm right down the street from you at the East Cleveland Cleaners. Please hurry. I will explain when you get here."

Rescued

When I saw my Aunt Sadie pull into the parking lot, it was a sight more beautiful than Christmas morning. I dashed out of the cleaners and jumped into her car.

"What are you wearing, boy?"

In my haste to get away, I completely forgot how awful this must've looked. As my eyes began to well with tears, I didn't have the words to explain to her. The only thing I could say was, "Please, Auntie, can we just go? Please go."

Riding back to her house seemed like an eternity even though it was just blocks away. I kept looking from side to side out of every window, thinking that at any second, my cousin could appear. My aunt was visibly nervous and confused. I was not sure if she was looking so concerned because she wanted to help me out of whatever trouble I was in, or if she wanted to put me out of her car because she didn't want anything to do with me.

We finally arrived at her house, and of course an explanation was due. I told her my story step by step, and all she could do was listen and cry with her hand over her mouth. "You have been through so much. I wish you would have called me sooner."

The funny thing was that with all the stuff going on, I never considered calling my dad's side of the family. I always felt like my dad was the only connection I had with them, and when he died, that connection was severed.

Even when my father was alive, we were considered the black sheep of the family. Yes, we were related, but my father's criminal activities were not looked upon favorably by his family. Although I hadn't done anything wrong as a child, I was like an extension of him. They were not close to him, so I was not close to them. The one thing that made me feel comfort was that they didn't view me the way I thought they did. My aunt was eager to help me out of the trouble I was in. With a hot meal every day and a warm place to sleep, I felt better than I had in a long time. All of the trouble and heartache seemed worth it if it landed me here. I just hoped it would last…

Aunt Sadie

My Aunt Sadie was a beautiful woman. She had fair skin and a slim figure for a lady in her early sixties. She'd been married a couple of times in her early years but never really had an interest in keeping a man around. It was just her and her dog Sweetie Pie, a German shepherd and the love of my aunt's life. Although I had so much trouble going on in my life, she opened her home up to me without batting an eye.

After a few months of stability, it didn't take long for Aunt Sadie to get full custody of me. Even though I was seventeen and nearly an adult, she was eager to help me transition into adulthood. She even helped me to get house arrest for the stolen car incident just months before. She had been an angel in my corner ever since I'd called her, and we were quickly bonding like the best of friends.

Being on house arrest gave us plenty of time to spend together, but staying in the house got old fast. We played cards, dominoes, and watched TV together all the time. House arrest meant I couldn't leave the house, but it didn't mean I couldn't have company. I had girlfriends from school coming and going all the time, and that was the only place we hit a snag. It was not that Aunt Sadie didn't want me to have company, it was just that she didn't trust young girls. She didn't think any of them were good enough for me. My girlfriends often made comments about how they thought my aunt and I were in a relationship because she hated them so much.

At seventeen, you couldn't tell me anything that would make me stop chasing girls. My hormones were completely out of control. I needed to have sex often and with as many girls as possible. Every time my aunt left out the front door, I was sneaking a girl in the back door. I hated sneaking girls into her house, but until I was off house arrest, that was the place it had to go down.

With only six days left before the end of my house arrest, the inevitable happened. My aunt caught me in the house having sex with a girl. My dumb ass knew she wasn't going to be gone long, and I went for it anyway. She put me on punishment for a month. *Punishment? I'm damn near grown and almost done with house arrest. Now I still can't leave the house.* It was like my house arrest was going to continue.

I felt bad that I'd disappointed my aunt because she had done so much for me and I knew how she felt about girls in her house. As much as I was abiding by her rules and abiding by the punishment, she was not relenting. Not being able to leave and not being able to have company was taking a toll on my sex life. I was nearly an adult, but nothing I said could put me back in her good graces. The punishment had lasted nearly a month, and something had to give.

Auntie had a hair appointment on Saturday, and I had to have sex or I was going to die. My girl Rachel lived two blocks away, and I knew I could sneak her in for some fun while Auntie was gone. Rachel was only fifteen, but her body was very mature. She was short, brown-skinned, and like most girls that young, she would do whatever I said. The moment Auntie hit the door, I was already on the phone. With Rachel living so close I knew she could be there lightning fast. As soon as I sneaked Rachel in the door, I felt that somehow I was going to get caught. However, nothing could come between me and my teenage hormones. Rachel and I handled our business, and I quickly rushed her out the back door. *Maybe all of my worry was for nothing*, I thought.

As soon as Auntie hit the door, she was furious. "What little hoe did you have in my house?"

Dumbfounded by how she knew, I quickly began to deny it. "I didn't have nobody in here, Auntie, honest."

"You a damn liar. I had Ms. Linda next door watching the house, and she called me the minute the little hoe got here."

Clearly caught, I was both embarrassed and irritated. "I'm sorry, Auntie, but it was the only way I could see my girlfriend."

"Your girlfriend? Which one? I get confused with all the little hoes you got running around and calling all the time. Not only are you grounded for another month, but now I'm taking away the telephone."

I was so pissed off I couldn't even muster up a reply. I just ran upstairs to my room and slammed the door.

"And don't be slamming no damn doors around here, either. I'm the only one can slam doors around my damn house," she yelled up the stairs.

You know what? I'm grown. I'm not about to sit up in the house with no phone and no pussy. I'm packing my shit and getting the hell out of here. I didn't know where I was going to go, but I had to get the hell out of there. I was off house arrest and two months away from my eighteenth birthday. I would just have to be a runaway for two months, and then I would be on my own legally.

I slowly and quietly packed my stuff up through the night. When I left to go to school that morning, I was leaving for good. I knew it would break Aunt Sadie's heart that I had to leave that way, but I couldn't live like that anymore. I was like a caged animal. Once I'd had a taste of freedom being on my own, I couldn't go back to structure. *I'm out!*

Grow Up Fast

I didn't have anywhere to keep my stuff, so I was going to drop my belongings off at my girl Rachel's house until I found a stable place to live. The minute I arrived at her door, I could tell something was wrong. "What's up, Rachel?"

Her eyes were red from crying. "I'm pregnant." Tears began to flow again.

All the blood rushed from my head and I felt like I was going to lose my balance. "Oh my God, are you sure?"

"Yeah, I'm sure. What are we going to do? I can't tell my parents. They are going to kill me."

"I know, I know, but maybe we should keep it a secret until I can figure something out."

My reassurance did little to stop her emotion. "I'm only fifteen and you're only seventeen. I just messed up my future. I know this is going to end bad, I just know it."

Sleeping in the Jungle

"Listen, I got your back. I'm going to have to go away for a while to hide out until I turn eighteen. In the meantime, I will figure out something."

Rachel looked like she'd just seen a ghost and quickly pleaded, "No, please don't leave me. You can't go and leave me by myself to go through this alone."

"I'm not leaving you, Rachel, I swear. But I'm a runaway. I have to go."

"Well, where are you going to go?"

"I don't know."

"Why don't you hide out here?"

"How the hell am I going to hide out here when you live with your parents? Don't just say stupid shit."

"Look, I have the upstairs all to myself, and my parents never come up there. I can sneak you in at night, and you can sneak out in the morning."

As much as it sounded like a ridiculous plan, it was a better plan than I had. I had nowhere to go, and at least this way I could help Rachel out with the pregnancy. Considering that I was homeless again, it didn't take me long to agree. I wasn't sure if we were going to get away with it, but it was worth a shot.

Eighteen and Ready

After hiding out for a couple of months at Rachel's, I celebrated my eighteenth birthday rubbing her stomach. I could feel my baby moving inside her. As my seed grew, I felt more and more worthless. *What will I ever have to offer a child without a pot to piss in or a window to throw it out of?* I had to get my shit together, and the only thing I knew how to do was hustle. I headed back over to my hood and I hit the block hard. I needed to provide for my child by any means necessary. I would go to school during the day, hustle in the evening, and sneak into Rachel's house at night. It was a truly dysfunctional arrangement, but it worked.

Rachel's parents finally found out that she was pregnant. Her stomach was beginning to show so much that they were bound to figure it out anyway. Her parents were devastated, and so was she. They were demanding to meet with me, but I didn't know what to say to them. All I could do was reassure them that I would be there for Rachel and the baby. I could assure them I would provide for their grandchild no matter what. I would do everything in my power to make sure Rachel still pursued her future. As soon as I finished reassuring them of all those things, they were looking at me like they didn't believe a word of it. They were so upset that they really didn't want to look in my direction. The moment the conversation was finally over, I said my goodbyes, walked out the front door, then sneaked around through the side door and up to our room. Her parents were upset about the fact that their daughter was pregnant, but they would've been more enraged if they knew I'd been living with them for the past seven months.

•••

Wow, this is really happening. Rachel's water broke while she was at school. My heart was beating out of my chest as I reached the hospital. I was really going to be a father. What would my child look like? I prayed she would be healthy. The doctor said the baby would be healthy at every doctor's appointment, but you wouldn't really know until the baby arrived. *What are they going to want me to do when I got there? I don't have the stomach for that kind of stuff. I probably shouldn't watch the birth.*

The moment I got into my scrubs to go into the operating room, I heard a cringe-inducing scream. Rachel was in excruciating pain. I knew childbirth was painful, but she was looking like she was not going to make it.

She screamed as another contraction hit her. Although it seemed like the baby was on the way out, the doctor kept warning her not to push. I was nervous as hell. I felt sorry for the pain Rachel was in, but I was anxious to see the baby. Finally, the doctor was ready to play ball. Rachel was finally dilated enough that it was safe for the baby to pass through.

The doctor raised his hand and said, "On my cue, one, two, three, push."

Holy shit, I see the top of a head. This had to be the most beautiful and disgusting thing I'd ever seen.

"One, two, three, push."

Rachel screamed.

"Oh my God, I can see the whole head now. It's the head!" I screeched in amazement.

Now that the head was clear, the doctor made two slight adjustments, and out came a screaming, bloody, pink-skinned, hairy baby girl.

I knew she was just a newborn, but that little girl had some lungs on her. That cry meant our child was alive. That cry meant our child was healthy. That cry also meant I was a father. Everything she would become was my responsibility. If I failed her, my life was a failure. She was my number-one priority and I had absolutely nothing positive going for me. It was time to get my life in order, but at eighteen, what in the world did that look like?

Unlikely Angel

When I left the hospital, I walked and stared off into space like a zombie. I just kept replaying the visual of what I had witnessed. I couldn't believe that little angelic face. A six-pound, eleven-ounce angel radiating with innocence. *Does she know her father is a teenage loser? No, she doesn't. I have one goal. I need to make something out of myself before she can see me for who I am.* At the time I was a loser, but she was too young to know. I was on a mission to give my little girl the best life, but I had to figure out how.

As I sat on the stairs of Jamison Middle School by myself, I slowly began to talk to God. "Lord, you know my heart is good even when my actions are not. I need Your help. I just need to be able to provide for this little angel You blessed me with. Can You please help, Lord? Please?" The tears began to flow.

Sleeping in the Jungle

As I was crying and holding my face with my hands, I could hear a voice slowly coming from the side of the building. "Why yo' little punk ass over here crying?"

This was not exactly the word from the Lord that I was looking for. In fact, it was the opposite of the Lord. It was Black, the local drug dealer who'd helped me out back when I was homeless.

"You supposed to be a drug dealer, and every time I see you, you looking sad like a little bitch."

"Man, fuck you, Black. You always talking shit! I'm not in the mood today, bruh. Just leave me alone."

"What's up, man? Somebody up here fucking wit you?"

"Naw, man, I just became a father today." Starting to fight for words through my tears I continued, "You hear what I said, I'm a fucking father and I don't have nothing. No money. Nowhere to live. Nothing. I'm fucked up out here, man, and I gotta figure some shit out, so just leave me alone. Like I said, today is not the day to fuck with me, okay?"

Unmoved by my testimony, Black just listened and finally sat down on the step next to me and threw his arm around me. "Look, little bruh, I know how you feel. You wanna sit here feeling sorry for yourself, or you gon' come work for me?" As I looked up dumbfounded, Black reached in his pocket and handed me a half ounce of dope. "Here, sell this off, and you should have about a thousand bucks. Listen, you can have that. Call me when you're done, and I'm gon' put you to work. If you fuck it up, you're on your own."

As quickly as he appeared, he walked away and was gone. *What the fuck just happened?* I was sitting there with about a hundred dollars to my name, and now I had a thousand dollars' worth of drugs. *Hell yeah!* Black was all right with me. I could hardly believe my luck. I was able to go and get some Pampers and a car seat for my baby to come home in from the hospital. I believed it was an amazing stroke of luck, because

I didn't believe the Lord would have sent this crazy fool to answer a prayer, but He does work in mysterious ways.

Outta Here

I couldn't tell you how happy I was to be able to do exactly what I promised Rachel's parents that I would do. My daughter's name was Laura. I loved this little girl with all that I was. She was almost six months old, and I was still able to sneak into Rachel's house every night and let my baby sleep on my stomach. She had gotten to the point where she couldn't sleep until she could listen to her daddy's heartbeat. I wanted the best for her, and I would die trying. She was slowly beginning to mutter "Da-da, da-da," as I made her laugh on the bed. When I snuggled up next to Rachel and Laura, I couldn't help but thank God that I could be with her as she grew up, and the three of us slowly drifted off to sleep.

"WHAT THE HELL IS THIS? WHAT THE HELL YOU DOIN' IN MY HOUSE?"

Rachel and I were jolted awake as her father stood in the doorway of her room.

"Uh, Daddy, it's not what you think?"

"The hell it ain't what I think. I think you got this nigga laying in yo' bed. You are just sixteen years old, little girl, and you are still under my roof. As for you, get your shit and get the hell outta here."

He had every right to be angry. The jig was up, and I had to go. For some reason in our teenage minds, we had never factored in a plan for the possibility that we might get caught. I had been living at her house for over a year. Did we think it was going to last forever? Well yeah, I guess we did. How stupid of us.

Sleeping in the Jungle

I gathered my things and headed for the exit, but Rachel was in complete panic mode wondering what she was going to do without me there anymore. I shared her regret, because how would baby Laura sleep without hearing her daddy's heartbeat? How would I sleep without feeling her moving on my chest? This really had been a long time coming. I had to make a way for myself and provide a home where there would be no fear of us being separated. I was determined to make a way.

Sympathetic to my plight, Black arranged for me to move into one of his drug houses. The drug house was cool, but there was always traffic in and out of the house. The best thing about this situation was that I could make money all day and night. No one could understand why I continued to go to school every day. I only had a few classes remaining until I could get my high school diploma. I was not sacrificing that for anything or anyone. After all, I'd promised my dad I would finish school, and I wanted my little girl to have a father she could be proud of.

Black and I made a hell of a team. He was as proud of having me as a protégé as I was to have him as my mentor. Black could also be a bad influence at times, though. He was always coming into the house with lots of girls, strippers, weed, and booze. It was a nonstop party around him, and it was impossible for me not to indulge. After being around Black's lifestyle, I was beginning to run through more girls than he was. My relationship with Rachel was becoming more and more of a distant memory. Although we never officially called it quits because of baby Laura, she could see the writing on the wall.

Sugar Hill

It was amazing how much Black was like my dad. My dad always had a vision of a father-and-son hustling team. Black was very protective of me, and everyone in the hood knew I was with him. I hadn't seen Dee since I'd run from his house over a year ago, but even he knew not to mess around with me now that I was with Black. We were making good money, but for some reason the drugs were drying up on the streets. Whenever you heard about a large drug bust in the news, it was only a matter of time before local dealers felt the effects in the hood.

The FBI announced that they had busted an international pipeline of cocaine that ranged from Mexico to the Midwest. Trying to find drugs during that time was nearly impossible, and I could tell that Black was getting anxious. There were stories out there about how easy it was to find drugs up in New York City, but nobody we talked to was willing to make the trip. Everyone who pretended to have a clue about it referred to the place to go as Sugar Hill. These guys had seen too many movies. All the old gangsters used to sell drugs in Sugar Hill, so I didn't consider that to be helpful at all.

Black did not seem to share my skepticism, and I didn't like the gleam in his eye. It seemed like he was talking about Sugar Hill daily and was continuing to gather information about it. "I got it, I got it! One-Fortieth and Broadway. My homey from across town told me that's where you get the shit, and it's in the heart of Harlem, better known as Sugar Hill, baby."

"Okay, congratulations," I said sarcastically.

"What the hell you mean, congratulations? We are going!"

"Going where?" I said nervously with my eyebrows raised.

"Sugar Hill, nigga. Where you think?"

"You must be crazy! I'm not going nowhere, bruh. Forget it."

I can't believe I let Black talk me into trying this dumb shit. I knew he had big aspirations, and the only reason I agreed to do it was because it was never going to work. I told him that my cousin had tried this before and he'd gotten robbed, but Black wasn't moved. I comforted myself by thinking we were going to ride all the way to New York, strike out, and come back home with our tails between our legs. Hell, there was nothing wrong with a road trip. Shit, I'd never even been out of Cleveland.

NYC, Baby

We rode down Interstate 80, and I had a painful feeling in my gut. *What if something goes wrong?* I was going to make sure that nothing happened to Black. "Black, where are we supposed to go once we get to New York?"

"Shit, I don't know. We just gon' roll into Harlem and ask where Sugar Hill at."

I knew for a fact that this was a flawed plan, but no matter what, we were going to make this happen. Black believed we were inconspicuous inside his grandmother's old white 1984 Ford Fairlane, but there was no way to get past the fact that we had Ohio license plates. *Cocaine is a powerful drug! We must be out of our minds to take this type of risk to score some of this white powder.* A lot of people may have made the trip successfully, but many had failed. The excitement in Black's eyes would have led you to believe that there was no risk at all. That could not be further from the truth. In fact, we were risking our lives. Although I shared in his excitement, there was a part of me that was scared to death.

The seven-hour journey from Cleveland to New York City seemed like it took forever. Not only was the ride extremely long, but his grandmother's car didn't have a tape player. As we rolled through country mountains and back roads, we were constantly scrolling through radio stations looking for any inkling of something familiar for us to hear.

"Roll something up, lil' Dave. Let's smoke."

"Hell yeah, I need to smoke to get my mind off this damn radio."

It had been my idea to grab some good weed before we made the journey. I didn't smoke weed, but if I was going to jail or die, I at least wanted to be high. In all actuality, my life was already screwed. If I didn't have Black, I was as good as dead anyway. I looked on the bright side—it was too late to turn back now.

Oh shit, we made it! NYC, baby. Crossing the George Washington Bridge was our last step before we reached Harlem. We'd come this far, but we still had a long way to go before we reached our goal. I'd never seen so many tall buildings before in my life. This had to be the most intimidating city in the world. It also seemed to be the most compelling. There were people everywhere walking, driving, and there was a never-ending stretch of stores. We were there, but we really didn't have a plan. The only thing we knew was to go to 140th and Broadway and ask where Sugar Hill was. The funny thing was, as we were approaching Broadway, there seemed to be dozens of people standing on street corners trying to flag us down. *What the hell is going on?*

Finally, we got to 140th and Broadway.

"Pull over right here, Black."

"I'm not pulling over in front of all these muthafuckas."

"Why, man? This is the spot, and everybody is flagging us down."

"Fuck it, crack the window but don't roll it down all the way."

Five black guys walked over to the car speaking a mile a minute, but none of them were speaking English.

"Yo man, we speak English," I said through the cracked window. The only thing I could make out as other guys surrounded the car was, "How much you need?"

"I got what you need," they all said in unison.

"Man, pull off, Black. Let's get the hell out of here."

Black must've been reading my mind, because before I got the words out, we were heading down the street.

"What the fuck was that?" I asked.

"I don't know, but it was crazy as hell. We have to come up with a different game plan."

Although the guys on the corner looked like regular black people, they were Dominican. I had never seen a Dominican before, but they resembled people from my neighborhood. They were all speaking Spanish and it was obvious they had what we wanted, but how were we going to get it if we couldn't communicate? We were frustrated as hell, but our first order of business was to find someone who spoke English.

We decided to go to a street called St. Nicholas to park and clear our heads. No better way to clear my head than to roll up a joint, because my nerves were about to jump out of my body.

Please God, don't let us die in this crazy-ass city. Please let us get what we came for so we can get the hell out of here.

It felt funny praying while we were smoking marijuana and looking to buy cocaine, but I couldn't think of a bad time to say a prayer. The marijuana smoke filled the car and started to seep out of my cracked window.

A man walked by, took a deep sniff, and said, "Damn, that smells good."

I quickly rolled down the window and said, "Yo man, you speak English? Where Sugar Hill at?"

He laughed and cautiously approached the car. "Look, fellas. You can't ride around Harlem with out-of-town plates asking where Sugar Hill is. You guys have to be crazy. You are in Sugar Hill right now, but you need to be a little more discreet. What y'all looking for?"

"A kilo."

Stunned by the answer, the stranger said, "Y'all sitting on the side of the road smoking weed with no destination, looking to buy a kilo? They say God takes care of fools and babies, and y'all don't look like babies. Get off this damn road and meet me at Gorgeous Restaurant a couple of streets up. I will make sure you get what you need."

As we drove away, I felt as uneasy as ever. "Black, are you sure we should trust this guy?"

"Hell no! Let's park a block away and walk to the restaurant. That way we can feel things out before we try to deal."

It seemed like a reasonable plan, except for the fact that we would be on foot walking up with $25,000 in cash on us. It almost seemed smarter to take our chances in a vehicle, but our Ohio plates were a dead giveaway. Approaching the restaurant, my nerves were in my asshole. You know you're in an anxious situation when your asshole has a heartbeat. Something didn't feel right, but we'd come too far to turn back, and considering the only plan we'd had was to drive seven hours and ask for Sugar Hill, things were going as well as could be expected.

●●●

The restaurant was packed with people. How the hell were we going to do a drug deal in a crowded restaurant? I knew we were from Small City,

USA, but that seemed brazen even by New York standards. As we took a seat, we didn't see the English-speaking Dominican anywhere. The one thing we recognized was that everybody in this restaurant seemed to be looking at us. *Damn! It's crazy how everybody knows we are completely out of place. Shit, are we wearing out-of-town license plates on our chests?*

I tapped Black's shoulder and leaned over to whisper, "There he goes right there."

"Yeah, I see him. Sit back and be cool."

As he approached us, I saw he had three other guys with him, and they didn't act as easy and friendly as he did. They were older men with olive skin who had no-nonsense looks. The men stopped approaching just feet from our table but hadn't acknowledged either of us. They were speaking Spanish, and although we didn't understand a word, they were obviously talking about us. Their dialect was foreign, but their body language was familiar in the world of drug dealing. They were trying to assess if this was a setup. I noticed the frustration on Black's face just seconds before he abruptly stood up and walked over to the men talking.

"What's up?" He stood face to face with them and stared into each of their eyes. *My goodness, why did he do that?* All three men halted their chatter and tried to decipher the provocativeness of the out-of-towner. They stared at each other in silence for a few seconds, although it felt like an eternity. *I thought my asshole was vibrating before, but now it feels like it's breakdancing.* I had completely lost control of my bowels. I barely noticed that I'd let out a series of small farts that were destroying the food aroma in this restaurant.

One of the strangers asked Black, "How old is your *hermano*?"

"He's eighteen."

In that moment, our New York friend walked over and asked me how old I was.

Nervously, I answered in a shaky voice, "I'm eighteen years old, sir."

As the man walked back to Black and the other strangers, he said in English, "It looks about right. He says he's eighteen, even though he looks much younger. I've never seen a cop who looks eighteen before, so I think we can deal. Come with me." Black looked back and waved his hand for me to come, and our friend turned around. "No, he can stay here. Just you."

Black walked back over to me and leaned in to whisper, "Stay here. I got it from here."

"Naw, Black, don't go with them and leave me here. Fuck that."

"Don't worry, bro. It's best if you stay here anyway. If something goes wrong, somebody's got to be a witness to what happened!"

My eyes filled with tears, and I was so scared that my teeth began to chatter. I had reached the limit of how far I was willing to go, so I grabbed Black's arm with a vise grip. "No. I'm fucking serious, man. Let's go. Fuck the deal. It ain't worth it. Please don't go!"

You would have thought I'd never said a word to Black. He shook his arm out of my grip and promptly walked out of the restaurant with the men.

Help me, Lord, help me! I screamed on the inside as I sat at the table by myself. A waitress brought me food and drink that I didn't even order. I don't know if I didn't touch it because I was too scared, or if I feared it was poisoned. It had been nearly an hour since they'd left, and everybody in the restaurant was staring at me. Some were openly whispering about me as I sat there riddled with paranoia. Something was seriously wrong. *It doesn't take this damn long to buy some dope!* As one hour turned into nearly two, the overwhelming feeling of dread came over me. If Black didn't return, how would I get home? He had the car keys, and I couldn't walk back to Ohio. Would they even let me walk out of this restaurant alive? *I knew this was a bad idea. Why didn't he just listen to me? Why did he go with them? He is the only person I have in this world who gives a shit about me. If I don't have him, I may as well be dead.*

•••

I looked into the distance and saw the most beautiful sight I'd ever seen. It was Black standing in the entrance of the restaurant, waving for me to come on. I jumped out of my seat so fast that I nearly flipped the table over. As we made our way out of the restaurant and up the block toward the car, I saw that Black was a nervous wreck. "What the fuck happened? What took you so damn long? Did you get it?" I had a million questions, but Black wasn't answering any of them. I could barely keep up with him because he was walking so damn fast. "Man, you gon' say something?"

"Just come on, bro."

We finally reached the car, and he pulled off like a bat out of hell. We made our way back toward the George Washington Bridge, and Black pulled out a huge bag of dope and screamed, "WE IN THERE, MY NIGGA. WE GOT ON IN NYC. ROLL ONE UP, BECAUSE THE CITY IS ABOUT TO BE OURS."

"Yo, you gotta tell me what happened? What took you so long?"

"Lil bro, they walked me down a small alley to a building just steps away from the restaurant. The hallway was dark and dingy with the strongest smell of urine you could imagine. Our New York friend asked to see the money, so I reached in my pants and pulled out the bag with the cash. The moment I showed that cash, I let them know I meant business."

"No shit, what did you say?"

"I told them don't think I'm green just because I'm going along with this shit so easily. You may have a lot of out-of-town suckers come through here, but I'm not one of them. If anything happens to me, my lil brother, or this cash, we gon' be the last people you ever rip off. Now, I showed you mine. Let me see yours."

"Get the hell outta here. You lucky they didn't kill yo' black ass. What did they say?"

"All of them laughed, but only one responded. Gon' tell me it's no need to give a speech because they do business straight for people who want to deal straight. I said, 'Well, that's me.'"

"I know that shit, right? You crazy as hell for going with them dudes. I thought I would never see yo ass again. I was sitting in that restaurant praying and pooting."

Black started laughing and swerving in the road.

"I swear to God that's my last joke. You have to pay attention to the road. How did the deal go down, fool?"

"Okay, you're right. As far as the deal, they wanted to count the money before they would show me the shit. We had the hallway steps filled with twenty-five stacks of a thousand. After we finished counting the money, they wanted to put it back in the bag. Then you won't believe what happened!"

"What?" I asked in a light voice.

"One of the old men pulled out a roll of duct tape, ripped off a strip, and started walking toward me."

"WHAT? Oh, I'm sorry! I meant what?"

"Lil bro, when I tell you my heart dropped, I thought it was about to be on in that hallway, because I ain't going out like that."

"Well, why the hell did he pull out the duct tape?"

"Man, he only wanted to tape up the bag so I couldn't go back in it and take money out while they went to get the shit."

"Wow."

"I was tripping because all three of them left, and I was standing there forever holding the taped-up bag. Just as I was thinking about leaving, they came back down the stairs and handed me the shit."

"Unbelievable, bro!"

"Yo, and this is the kicker. When I looked in the bag, I noticed it was more than what we paid for. The old man said something in Spanish, and our New York friend translated. He said for me to consider the extra coke a reason to come back and see him. He tossed me a phone number, and we all walked out of the building."

"That was the sickest story I ever heard."

I only wanted to make it out of there alive. I never imagined that we'd not only get what we came for, but we would leave that with a connection that could serve as a pipeline of cocaine to our starved city. As we made our way through the mountains of Pennsylvania, I knew that everything was about to change.

Becoming a man

Prom Night Massacre

I never imagined things would work out so well. Black and I were rolling in cash. We made the trip to New York every other week, and there wasn't a single drug dealer in Cleveland who wasn't looking to connect with us. We were the only guys in town with the dope, but that wasn't always a good thing. When you are the only ones with it, the cops and the robbers see that too. The best thing about Black was that he had street credibility. People knew he was not to be fucked with. Me, on the other hand—the hood would like to take chunks out of my ass any opportunity they got. It was a good thing I had Black for protection. Not only was he my partner in crime, but he was also like my father. He made sure I had what I needed for school, a nice car, and a place to live. The word on the streets was clear. I was Black's right hand. If you fucked with me, you fucked with him.

•••

This was the best time in my life since my father was murdered. I could have and do anything I wanted. I was headed toward graduation, and I knew I could convince Black to buy me a new car as a present. I left the

Sleeping in the Jungle

tuxedo shop with a fresh white tux for prom, and you couldn't tell me shit. However, I was headed to meet Black to give him a little bad news. I got so wrapped up in the prom festivities that I forgot it was the week we were supposed to drive back to New York for another shipment. I was going to tell Black that we needed to push it to the following week, because there was no way I was missing my prom.

"What's up, lil homey. You ready to ride out?"

"Yo, Black, I completely forgot to tell you that I have prom this weekend."

Black responded angrily, "What the fuck you mean, you forgot to tell me? Do you understand what we're involved in here?"

Shocked by his sharpness, I said, "Yo, I swear I didn't do it on purpose. I just thought we could push it to next week."

Finally calming down, he came to his senses and let me off the hook. "Sometimes I forget how young you are. You go ahead and enjoy the prom. We can make the trip next week, no problem."

When I got back from the barber shop, I could hardly believe my eyes. The transport car that we used for shipping

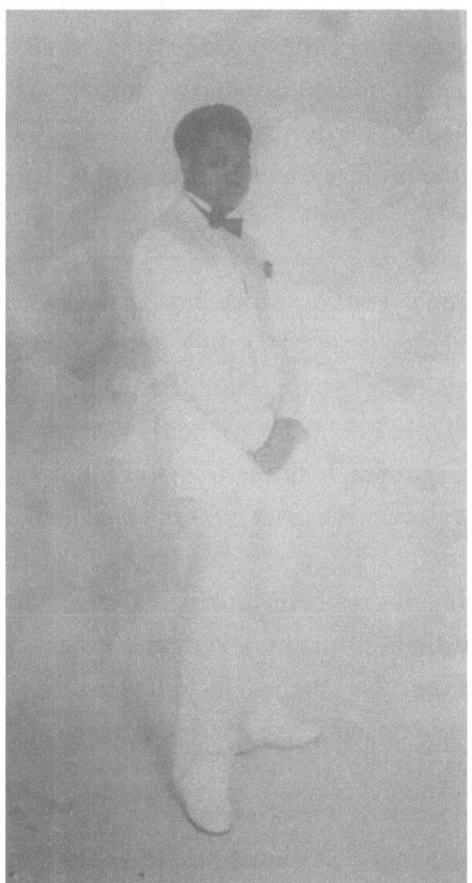

He think he clean

the drugs was gone. *Oh no, he didn't! He went without me. How could he do that? We had a system.* We always made it through because it looked like him and a little kid on vacation. *What the hell was he thinking?* I couldn't let that bother me, though. This was my prom weekend, and I was about to get high and have sex for three days straight. I knew Black had everything covered.

I was going to the prom without a date like a true player. I didn't want to give any of my girlfriends an advantage over any other, so I was not taking anyone. I wasn't going in a limo either. I was driving the new car Black bought me as a graduation present. It had two fifteen-inch subwoofers in the trunk and 72-spoke Dayton rims. I pulled into the prom looking completely out of the ordinary, and everybody was tripping on how crazy I was. I was high as hell, didn't have a date, and bumping sounds out the trunk.

I walked into the ballroom, and everything looked nostalgic. There were huge crystal chandeliers hanging from the ceiling, and the table décor was white and gold. Everyone was laughing and dancing in a sea of pressed suits and nice dresses. Once I made my rounds to everyone's table cracking jokes, I saw my friend Sarah sitting by herself looking like a hot mess. Her makeup was all over the place, and she looked like somebody took a shit in her coffee.

"What the hell is wrong with you over here, looking like a retired disco queen?" I admit it wasn't the best-quality joke, but I expected somebody to chuckle. Nobody at the table laughed, including Sarah.

One of my classmates leaned over and whispered in my ear, "She got stood up for prom."

I instantly felt like shit. Once Sarah saw my classmate whisper into my ear and my facial expression changed, she burst into tears and ran out of the building. *Damn, how stupid of me!* It was all my fault, so I didn't allow anyone to go after her, because that was my job. As she ran into the parking lot, I matched her stride for stride. After all, she wasn't just my classmate—she was one of my closest friends. She was the one who voluntarily did my schoolwork when I was homeless. She was there for me then, and I needed to be there for her now.

When I finally caught up to her, I could hardly find the words, so I had to try to make light of the moment. "I will never forgive you if you make me slip in these patent leather shoes and bust my fucking lip."

She let a laugh slip through her tears as she muttered, "Shut up, punk."

"Look, to hell with that dude who stood you up. That was his loss. Come on over to my car and let's talk for a minute, or do you want to just stand here in the parking lot looking stupid?" Once in my car, I sparked up a joint. "You want to hit this?" I asked jokingly, knowing she was a square.

"Yeah, fuck it!"

In utter disbelief, I passed it to her, and she hit it. Then she hit it again.

"Hey, slow down, girl. You're new to this. I can't be responsible for you running through the prom naked."

In an instant, she burst out laughing.

"Now that's the Sarah I know!"

She finally began to compose herself. "Thank you so much, Dave."

"Let's go back in there together and enjoy the rest of the night. I'm glad your date didn't show up, because now I have the prettiest date at the prom."

"You don't have to do that, Dave. I'll be fine."

With a huge grin on my face, I said, "I know I don't have to do it. I want to! Plus, if I show you a good enough time, you might give me a shot of pussy."

She punched me. "Shut up."

We got out of the car and walked back into the prom arm in arm.

Everyone looked at us like we just stepped out of the Twilight Zone. We spent the rest of the night laughing, dancing, taking pictures, and having the time of our lives.

As the night ended, Sarah looked at me through the clearest and happiest eyes I had ever seen. "Thank you so much, Dave. I will never forget what you did for me tonight. I love you and I always will!"

I left the prom and headed back to the hood. I felt like a million bucks. I saved the night for one of my closest friends. If I'd gone with Black on a drug run, I would not have been there for her. There was no doubt that I made the right decision by not going. The Lord uses us all in different ways; I was just glad that he used me to help Sarah.

•••

I woke up the next day feeling weird. It was not just that I was still high and drunk from prom. I hadn't heard a word from Black. The moment after I thought about him, the phone rang. It was Black! "What's up, fool? Where the hell you at?" I asked.

He paused for a quick second and said, "Game over, little bro! We got stopped on the freeway with the shit. The cops are going to be coming soon. Take care of my baby!" Then he hung up abruptly.

"Oh my God," I screamed. No, not again! Black had taken the place of the father I lost. I was losing my father again. "Oh my God," I screamed again. "Help." The tears began to flow.

I knew it was not a joke. "Take care of my baby" was the secret code to clean out all our stash houses. *This is really happening. Wait a minute. I know God used me to bless Sarah at the prom, but did the Lord use the prom to save me also? If I hadn't turned down the trip for prom, I would have been arrested with Black. What in the world is going on? Why on earth does the Lord keep stepping in to save me?*

Graduation Mourning

Not only did I lose my best friend, father figure, and confidant, but my grandmother passed away the same morning. Just hours after I got the fateful call from Black, she passed peacefully in her sleep. Even though I didn't have a close relationship with my grandmother, I felt a deep mourning for her. She survived cancer, diabetes, both legs being amputated, and the loss of her sight. She fought through all those heartbreaks, but she couldn't survive the thought of losing her home. When my cousin lost the money from her second mortgage, she had difficulty keeping up with the higher payments. She slowly fell further and further behind, and the bank was eventually going to take the house.

As if my sense of loss wasn't enough, the bad breaks just kept coming. My grandmother's funeral was going to be the same day as my high school graduation. There was really no decision to be made; I had to pay my respects to my grandma. Even though I wouldn't be walking the stage with my classmates, I still fulfilled my promise to my dad. I was a high school graduate and I knew he was rejoicing in heaven. I wished I could rejoice with him, but my life was spiraling out of control.

The day of the funeral was truly somber. My grandmother had been in her eighties, and I had no idea how many people knew her. The funeral home was packed with friends and family there to pay their last respects. It took forever to reach the casket for the viewing because the line was so long, but when I got there, I was pleased. She looked so peaceful lying in the casket. In every memory I had of her, she was always angry. On that day, she was finally able to rest. I kissed my hand, touched the casket, and turned only to stop dead in my tracks. I was standing face to face with my mom.

"Hello, son."

I hadn't seen my mom in years. My face lost all of its color. My lips turned crackhead white. I tried to think of something to say but drew a blank. Her eyes looked as if she had been crying for days. It took me so long to find words that I came to the realization that I couldn't think of any. All I could do was reach both arms forward and pull her to my chest in a gentle hug while mouthing a single word: "Momma."

Our embrace seemed like it went on forever. She hugged me back, but she held me as if the hug was unexpected. Once I released her from my grasp, I told her I was so sorry for her loss and I knew how hard it must be. She was listening intently, but I could see that she was surprised by the warm reception.

"David, I thought you would be mad at me."

"I was mad at you, and I may still be mad at you, but I haven't seen you in so long that I'm just happy to see you."

My words caused her to collapse to her knees. I couldn't pick her up, so I just got on the floor with her, and we both wept and wept. "Please stop crying, Momma. Everything is going to be okay." I was able to walk her back to her seat, and I went outside for some fresh air.

Outside of a few extra pounds, my mom looked the same as the last time I saw her. She was beautiful. I wanted to be mad at her, but for some reason I couldn't find an ounce of anger. I forgave her without realizing that I had. I was a grown man and I knew she'd done the best she could. I wanted to give her the grace I hoped the Lord would give me. It was good to see her healthy and safe, and I was thankful I was able to free her from the judgment she thought I would unleash on her.

We left the funeral on good terms and she informed me she would be staying in town for a week to handle Grandma's affairs. I believe we both got the closure we needed the day we reunited. We said we would stay in touch, but for some reason, it never happened.

Sleeping in the Jungle

Eaton

My mom was handling my grandma's affairs, but I had affairs of my own to tend to. Now that Black was gone, I was a marked man. Every thug for a hundred miles was looking to rob me because they suspected that Black left me a rich man. Black did leave me about $25,000, but the hood perception was that he left me a million. I didn't know what the hell I was going to do. My pager wouldn't stop going off for sales, but I didn't know who to trust anymore. I didn't have the product to sell them anyway. The last thing I was going to do was risk going to New York and end up with the same fate as Black.

I decided to reach out to my childhood friend Eaton. We grew up on the same street, and although he was a couple of years older than me, we were really good friends. Eaton was a very large man and that was where he got his name. He was always eating, so we began to call him Eaton. His body was very disproportionate. His face and legs were the appropriate size for a man about 5'10", but his stomach was not the right size for any man. His belly looked like he was twenty-five months pregnant. I'd never seen anyone with a stomach like that. He always looked uncomfortable. He wobbled when he walked, massaged the steering wheel with his stomach as he drove a car, and if he was to ever use your bathroom to do number two, your toilet would never be the same.

Although Eaton was not Mr. Universe by any means, he knew how to sell drugs better than the best of them. He could step out on the block with ten bucks in his pocket, and by the end of the week he could have ten grand. His hustle hand was real. When I told him about my dilemma with getting drugs into the city, he was eager to assist. He said he had a cousin who lived in Texas who'd been working with a Mexican cartel for many years. Even though we were not on that level, he was sure his cousin would like to expand into the Midwest.

I was extremely nervous about making such a move. After all, if I couldn't transport dope from New York, how the hell was I going to get it back from Texas? Talk of Texas and Mexican cartels seemed way out of my league, but I didn't have anything to lose by hearing the man out. Plus, there was a part of me that was slightly intrigued, considering his cousin paid for our plane tickets to come down. My expectations were low, but I couldn't resist the free trip.

Texarcan

It was hot as hell when we got to Texas. You knew it was too damn hot when you could see the heat.

"Fuck, I thought the airport would have some better air conditioning," Eaton mumbled as we walked through the airport. It was hot, but I seemed to fare better than my pot-bellied friend. This fool was laboring so bad that I was ready to get him a wheelchair and push him the rest of the way.

"You should call your cousin and tell him that we landed."

"Don't worry, he has our flight information. I'm sure he's already here."

True to his word, his cousin was waiting for us in the baggage claim area. Except for the cousin being about ten shades darker, these guys were almost identical. That stomach must run in the family. Both of these pot-bellied fools needed to do about 150 million sit-ups. I didn't think I could enjoy my trip looking at those two big-ass bellies. If he was going to show us a good time, I hoped he didn't take us to the beach.

"Welcome to Houston, lil' cuz." Watching these guys try to hug through those stomachs was hilarious. "What's up. You must be Dave. You can call me Texarcan." He reached out for a handshake. He had a look of both surprise and curiosity when he looked at me. Before I could return his greeting and shake his hand, he quickly asked, "How old are you, little man? Where yo' daddy at?" Although he let out a smile, he must have seen that I was in no mood for jokes.

"I'm old enough to go to jail if you two fat niggas fuck this up."

He and Eaton burst out into laughter, and I saw that I earned his respect, but he had a long way to go before he earned mine. All the way to the hotel, I tried to tune out the continuous conversations these two were having about food. We were down there trying to make a drug connection, and all they were talking about was where to get every kind of meal imaginable.

What the hell am I doing down here? Is this the life that I want? I know it's not. After I make it back home, I need to do some soul searching. My father was killed over drugs, and Black is facing fifteen years in prison over the same shit. Now my dumb ass is down in Texas with the fat boys getting ready to meet a similar fate if I'm not careful.

It was no surprise that we grabbed something to eat before heading to the hotel. After everyone had eaten and gotten settled, it was time to get down to business.

"So Tex, I know you know our problem, so I'm anxious to hear how you can help us solve it."

"You guys really don't have a problem the way I see it. I got everything you need."

"What does that mean?"

"It means what I said. I got what you need. If you come down here to get the dope, I can give you a price of fourteen thousand per key, but if I bring them to you I will need twenty thousand per key."

Holy shit! We were paying $25,000 per key from New York and we were going to pick it up. This guy would bring them to us for $5,000 less. *This guy must be a gift from God or a fucking fraud.* I didn't know which one he was, but he definitely had my attention. "Fourteen thousand and twenty thousand seems a little cheap. I don't know how you guys do it in Texas, but our customers want a quality product, not that watered-down bullshit."

As soon as I finished my statement, Texarcan went into his backpack and pulled out two bricks of cocaine. "My shit is coming straight from Mexico, uncut! I got access to this 24/7! If you want it, I got it."

Eaton grabbed the packages and said, "Damn, cuz, you saying if I wanted to take these back on my own, I can have both of these keys for twenty-eight thousand?"

"That's exactly what I'm saying."

I quickly interjected. "Whoa, whoa, whoa, whoa. I need my work brought to me. I didn't say nothing about taking nothing back."

Irritated, Eaton said, "I didn't say nothing about you taking nothing back. These are mine. I'm willing to take the risk, so these belong to me."

"Oh, hell no. If you gon' drive them back to Ohio, you gon' be driving back by yourself."

Smiling, Eaton said, "I'm not driving shit back. I'm gon' strap these puppies under this big-ass belly and get on the plane."

Tex and I both looked at Eaton like he was out of his mind. "There is no way I'm flying on a plane with you and two keys. Are you crazy? If you're doing that, I don't know you. Don't say shit to me in the airport, on the plane, or getting off the plane. I'm not giving yo' fat ass a ride after the flight. You gon' need a cab or you can call you a ride. Either way, I'm not fucking with you."

Texarcan said, "If you gon' fly with them, I'm gon' need my twenty-eight thousand up front before you leave." They both burst out laughing.

•••

Sleeping in the Jungle

As we approached the airport to head home, I was carrying my balls in my back pocket. When your balls were in your back pocket, sitting down was extremely painful. Eaton, on the other hand, seemed to have balls made of cast iron. He went into the large woman's section at the mall to purchase two pairs of tights and was preparing to walk through airport security with two kilos snuggled under his belly. Outside of the fact that he was sweating profusely, you wouldn't think he had a care in the world. Sweating was not exactly uncommon in Texas, because it was a thousand degrees.

I purposely positioned myself about twenty people behind him as we went through airport security. If they grabbed this fool, my plan was to get out of line, rent a car, and just drive back home. I couldn't believe how calm this guy was. He was making small talk with people in line even though he was the next person to go through the metal detector. With one nod to the agent and zero alarms sounding as he went through the detector, he was off to his gate to board the plane.

Whew. I couldn't believe it! This fool had made it so far, but it was not over until he made it home. Boarding the plane, I didn't even look in his direction. I walked to my seat as if he were invisible. I hated to say that he was playing his part too well, but he was just way too comfortable. He must have really found comfort in food, because every time the stewardess walked past, he ordered something—chips, cookies, sandwiches, and vodka. If there was anybody on this plane who I thought was doing something illegal, it wouldn't be him.

There was a tremendous amount of relief on my face when we landed. I had to get off the plane and make it home before I shit on myself. I was so uptight you would've thought I had the dope. Although I would never take that kind of risk to pay $14,000, I was looking forward to Texarcan arriving with those $20,000 deals. It looked like I would be back in business.

Drop Down

Happy Birthday! Yeah, I was nineteen years old and starting to become a man. I had just grabbed a house in the suburbs and was moving dope out the door as fast as it was coming in. I had a team of people working for me, so it was very easy to escape the cops and robbers. Considering my father had preached about education, I decided to go further than high school. I enrolled in college. For some reason, college came very easily to me. I never paid much attention in high school, but my comprehension skills were always stellar. I even convinced my boy Jonesy to go to school with me. He was not much of a student, though. I think he only did it because I wanted him to.

Texarcan was making trips up here more often, and each time, he seemed to bring more and more drugs. Eaton and I were selling the drugs so fast that he wanted to start storing some of the dope at my house so he could cut down on his trips. Being young and naïve, I agreed just to please him and Eaton, but something was making me feel very uncomfortable. I had ten keys on my back porch that weren't even mine, and if the police came up in here I would never get out of prison. Eaton was dropping by the house all hours of the day and night to get drugs, and the traffic didn't look good in front of my neighbors. I really wanted to cut off the relationship, but I was in too deep.

The one thing I liked to do to pass time was play video games. On Saturdays, me, Jonesy, and Eaton got together for a Mortal Kombat competition. I won't say I always won, but I always won! Jonesy went for a quick beer run, so that gave me an opportunity to kick Eaton's ass one on one for a little while. After a few wins, I looked at the clock wondering where the hell Jonesy was with the beer. No sooner had I showed some concern than I heard him pull into the driveway. A few seconds later we heard a few loud thumps coming from the porch. Curious, I paused the game and we ran to look out the window. As we looked out, we saw Jonesy standing in the driveway talking with two guys.

"Who the hell is that out there with him?" Eaton asked.

"I don't know." Finally, I saw Jonesy reach down to pick up his wallet before the three of them began walking toward the entrance of the house.

"It's a robbery," Eaton proclaimed as we both ran back into the living room. I quickly flipped the couch over, where I had a small arsenal of weapons. I grabbed the most menacing weapon I could find, an AK-47. As the footsteps on the porch drew closer, I began to shake uncontrollably. "Yo, I'm scared, bro. I don't think I can shoot nobody!"

Eaton quickly grabbed the gun from my hand and said, "Well I can, because these muthafuckas are not coming in here. If they do, we are all going to die."

Scared out of my mind, I stood behind Eaton. As the key entered the door from outside, Eaton decided to beat them to the punch and quickly snatched the door open. They were so surprised that their eyes opened wide like they saw a ghost. We were all standing face to face. Me and Eaton on one side and Jonesy and the two men on the other.

Eaton quickly raised the gun up, and for some reason he rested the barrel of the AK on Jonesy's shoulder. He held the trigger with the other hand, and the robbers never saw the gun. "What's up, Jonesy?" Eaton yelled, but Jonesy was silent. Jonesy slowly began to fall inside the door as if he were collapsing, and one of the robbers raised a platinum silver pistol from behind Jonesy's back.

BANG! BANG! BANG! The three shots were so loud that they were deafening. We pulled a collapsed Jonesy from the doorway, and Eaton slammed the door shut as the robbers were fleeing.

"Jonesy, say something. Are you shot?"

Jonesy didn't reply, but he was moaning in despair as he dragged himself across the floor.

"Jonesy, are you hit?"

He slowly pulled himself up against the wall in an upright seated position while he continued to moan. Jonesy reached a shaking hand around his back to touch where the robbers had a gun pointed just moments ago. After reaching the spot where he felt a sensation, he brought his hand back around and saw it was blood-free.

"Jonesy, come on, man. Say something. Do you need an ambulance? Are you shot?"

He saw that his hand was blood-free and answered with a slow, "Naw."

"Man, get yo' ass up, asshole. Ain't nothing wrong with you. You moaning and sliding across the floor all dramatic and let the niggas get away."

The three of us laughed and we made a joke of the moment, but this was very serious. Somebody had just tried to rob and potentially kill us all. In that moment, I had what an alcoholic might call a moment of clarity. When I sold the rest of the dope I had in my possession, I was officially out of the game. *I'm going straight and leaving this life behind for good!*

Transition

The next day I met Eaton for breakfast to break the news to him. The moment he sat down at the table, I just got straight to the point. "I'm done, Eaton."

"Done with what? We haven't even ordered yet."

"Not done eating. I'm done selling dope."

"Why you gotta be so dramatic, lil' Dave? Robberies are a part of the game, bruh. If anything, we showed them not to fuck wit' us." His argument fell on deaf ears.

"I'm a schoolboy, man. I'm not a gangster. It's only a matter of time before some real gangsters come knocking. I gotta go my own way, and you and Tex can handle this without me. I will turn all my customers over to you. Just don't forget about me when you guys get rich."

Sad, Eaton finally relented. "I'm gon' miss you, lil' homey, and I promise I won't forget you."

Man, that was like a tremendous weight off my shoulders. I had less than a kilo left to sell before I was free. I had to abandon a nice house because the killers knew where I lived, but I could surely find another place to stay. Life was going to be strange without the dope game because it consumed every day of my life. College by day, and hustler by night.

It seemed easy to say that I was done with the game, but I had to figure out how I was going to make a living. I had never had a job; the only thing I'd ever done was hustle. I had about a hundred grand, so I could've started a little business. A clothing store, car wash, restaurant, or something like that. First thing's first, I had to get rid of the rest of the dope I had, then the future was mine.

Elle B. Six

Set Time

Losing Black had been catastrophic for me. His lawyers hadn't been able to negotiate anything less than fifteen years. However, he was in good spirits. Every time I talked to him, he seemed like he was accepting his fate and ready to do his time. I was so worried about Black that I hadn't begun thinking about my next move yet.

Riding through the hood, checking my trap spots, I saw a cookout that looked like it was jumping. I usually never participated in hood parties because there was always a set of scandalous niggas lurking in the shadows, but this party had cars lined all the way down the street. I was going to keep riding, but I thought maybe I would just drop in for a few quick seconds. That way I could get a drink, a rib bone, and check out some of the ladies.

When I walked through, there was beauty everywhere, but this was not my scene. I'd already seen too many people I didn't want to see. I made my way through just long enough to get what I came for: a drink and something to eat. After talking shit with a few people, I went back to my car and back to the hustle.

A couple of days later, my phone rang from a phone number I didn't recognize. "Hello?"

"What's up, Chinaman?" an unfamiliar voice said.

"Chinaman? I think you got the wrong number."

"No, I got the right number. My name is Kelli, and I saw you the other day at the cookout. As soon as I saw you I said you looked like a little Chinese man, so that's why I called you Chinaman. I hope you don't mind. I tracked down your number because I want to meet you."

"I don't have a number that's easy to track down. How did you get it?"

"Eaton gave it to me because I told him you were cute. So do you want to meet up or what, Chinaman?"

"Meeting up sounds cool, but you can call me by my name. David or Dave. What do you want to meet me for? I ain't nobody," I said with a slight laugh.

"I just thought you looked cute and I wanted to see if you wanted to meet up."

Now I'd been around long enough to know a sophisticated setup, but this was remedial. Who in the hell would be this obvious trying to sic a girl on me? Yeah, it might be a setup, but I was not running. The robbers might think that just because Black was gone they could keep coming at me full steam, but I was ready to fight for my respect. I was walking away from the game, but I wasn't going to walk away from my dignity. *When they spring the trap, I will be ready!*

"Yeah, Kelli. I want to kick it, but we have to meet up so I can see what you look like."

"Oh, you won't be disappointed."

"Of course you gon' say that. I don't expect you to say you're butt-ass ugly."

We both laughed and agreed to meet later that evening at a restaurant downtown where I felt comfortable. I had all my people in place. I had a hired gun inside the restaurant, in the parking lot, and on both ends of the block. When shit went down, I was gonna let these assholes have it. When my phone rang, my heart was pumping because I was ready to teach these fools a lesson. "Hey, what's up, girl?" I said as I playfully answered the phone.

"What's up, Chinaman? I'm in the parking lot. Are you coming out?"

"Yeah, I'll be out in a minute, but don't call me Chinaman."

This was it; playtime was over. I gave the signal as I walked out of the restaurant. Everything was in place. If somebody attempted to walk up to the car, my team was going to let loose. I was happy to see that the girl was alone in the car. I quickly glanced into the back seat to make sure there wasn't anybody crouched down. Once I got in the passenger seat, my boys would rush the car if they saw me take my hat off.

As I opened the door, I saw a petite young lady with the most beautiful eyes I'd ever seen. She was about 110 pounds soaking wet. I listened to her tell me she didn't want to come into the restaurant because her hair wasn't done while she adjusted her ball cap. There was something wrong here. This girl was way too articulate to be a part of a hood setup. Plus, there was a Bible on the back seat.

"So, what's up, lil' mama? You said you wanted to meet me, so here I am."

"Yeah, I wanted to meet you because you left the cookout before I got a chance to say hello. I hope you don't think I'm desperate or anything. I just really felt like I needed to know you."

I grabbed my phone to call Jonesy. "Yeah, I think I may be good, but keep the fence up on the house," I said in as close to a code word as possible before hanging up. "Well, if you need to know me, how are you going to do that if you don't want to go into the restaurant?"

"We can always get some food to go."

"That sounds like a plan, but get the food and go where?" I had to ask because I knew she didn't think it was that easy to find out where I lived.

"Wherever you want."

I suggested we take our meal down to Lake Erie to eat in the car and watch the waves. Although I was riding in the car with her, I had three cars following us because I still didn't fully trust it. As we arrived at the lake and shared our meal, I realized there was no scheme that would be this elaborate. This girl was only nineteen. She had a good job with no kids. She was raised in a religious family and she didn't have a boyfriend. Everything about her was too good to be true, because not only did she have all these attributes, she was drop-dead gorgeous. I had to trust my gut and allow my guys to go home. I stepped out of the car to throw our trash away and waved for the guys to go.

•••

In the days and months that followed, Kelli and I were inseparable. I had even taken over her vehicle because my car was too hot in the hood. I dropped her off at work and hustled all day before picking her up at the end of her shift. In just a short period, I got her to rent an apartment in Richmond Heights for me, and she practically lived with me. Although she was completely a church girl, she was mesmerized at the hint of danger and enjoyed being in a relationship with a criminal like myself. She loved the wild side, but her family did not share her enthusiasm. They did not want us together at all. Even though my drug-dealing days were coming to an end, they didn't know that. I didn't blame them, either. I wouldn't want my daughter to date someone like me, but they didn't have a choice. The two of us were in love, and there was nothing anybody could do about it. I was hoping I would grow on them once I began to legitimize myself.

Jerked My Life Away

The Jerk was a guy I'd known since I was about six years old. We always saw each other in the neighborhood and went to school together until around fourth grade. As the years went by, we weren't friends, but we were cool. Because we went to different high schools, we would sometimes trade clothes to try to always look like we were fresh. We sold dope on the same corner, but there was something about this guy's hustle that was disgusting. He was always broke and always catching a case. The guy had about five prison numbers at the age of nineteen. He used to make the block so hot. When the narcotics unit would raid our block, that fool would take off running because he had one rock and he didn't want to swallow it. He would rather run on foot, try to hide the rock, and spend a night in jail, because that rock signified the last twenty bucks he had to his name. I could not stand this guy. After he was released from prison for the ten thousandth time, he was looking for someone to front him some dope because he was leaking. Every hustler knew this type of guy quite well.

It just so happened that this Jerk ran into me on the right day. I was desperately trying to get rid of the rest of the drugs I had, so I decided to give him a quarter ounce of crack and told him he didn't owe me. Black had done the same thing for me when I'd been in dire straits, so I wanted to pay it forward. I didn't want to give him something smaller because I knew he would try to call me once he sold it. I was moving weight and I couldn't be bothered with small transactions like that. I really wanted him to just take the drugs, disappear, and I could feel like I did a good deed.

About a week later, the Jerk started paging the hell out of my beeper. He wanted to buy an ounce of dope for a thousand bucks. I told him I was in school and I would call him once I got out. I didn't even have a ride until school was out, and Kelli would come pick me and Jonesy up. Once school was out I knew I could shoot right to the hood and serve this fool, because I always kept a couple of ounces on me for just such an occasion.

However, once I got to the hood, he wasn't there. I called him, and he told me that he was walking down Harvard Avenue from his mother's house and asked if I could come and pick him up. Extremely irritated, I agreed.

As I drove up 142nd Street and arrived at Harvard Avenue, I made a right toward 144th. Once I reached the light at 144th, about twenty-five police cars began pulling out of the side street. My initial thought was, *The police about to show somebody some love,* but it soon caught my attention that all the cops seemed to have their eyes fixed on me. Recognizing this, I already had the car in reverse.

BOOM! A police car rammed me from behind. I looked over and saw the horror on Kelli's face and heard Jonesy's screams in the back seat. With all the commotion, the only thing on my mind was the two ounces of dope I had sitting on my lap. There was no way in hell I was about to let them arrest me with all that dope. In the words of my brothers and sisters from slavery, "A catching comes before the hanging."

I threw the car back in drive and zoomed around the opposite side of the small building that they came from. As we tried to make our escape, I was looking right into the eyes of a police officer who exited his car and had me directly in the sights of his gun. He would be completely justified if he fired and killed us all, but for some reason, as we locked eyes, he lowered his weapon. For some reason, he didn't fire. Probably because we all looked so young. Whatever the reason, the fact that he spared those shots meant there was a muthafuckin' police chase going on. As I rode around that building's parking lot, I busted through a chain-link fence on 144th, drove across the grass of Moses Elementary School, and it was off to the races.

I looked in the rearview mirror and saw what looked like the entire police department behind me.

"Please stop the car. Please?" Kelli bellowed.

I interrupted her screams and told her in clear words, "You crazy as hell. If I stop with these two ounces of crack on my lap, they gon' split it between all three of us and give us all a dope case."

You would not believe how my words hit their mark, because within seconds, she was leaning over on my lap working the horn so cars would get the hell out of the way. It felt like Bonnie and Clyde in an instant. I sped down 144th Street, and we arrived at Miles Road and hung a left. When I got to 147th I made another left, which was a bad move. "Fuck, a roadblock."

Thank God it was only one car. Luckily for us, he left enough space behind his vehicle for us to squeeze through. We zipped around his car before he could exit his vehicle. In his haste to rejoin the chase, he tried to pull off after us. His momentum was so slow that he blocked off the other pursuing cop cars. By the time I made it up 147th and reached Harvard again, we were by ourselves. No cop cars in sight. As I whizzed up Harvard Avenue, I was able to throw the dope out the window in the midst of the traffic. Once I had disposed of the drugs, there was no longer any reason to continue fleeing and jeopardizing our lives. I pulled into the BP gas station on Lee Road, put the car in park, and awaited my arrest. My arrogance led me to believe that my arrest would simply come with a set of cuffs, but to my surprise the cops decided to throw in a side order of ass-whippin'!

Bloodied and battered as we arrived at the Fourth District Police Station for booking, I couldn't help but wonder if the Jerk set me up. My homey since third grade? My homey I used to share clothes with? The homey I just gave $250 of my hard-earned crack to for free simply because he just got out of jail? No way. When the cops got me in their office, they didn't even try to hide how they got me. One of them even had a file on his desk with the Jerk's name on it, followed by the initials CI for CONFIDENTIAL INFORMANT.

Wow. I couldn't believe the Jerk had set me up.

Finally Caught Up

"Y'all ain't got shit on me," I arrogantly blurted out. As much as they hated it, they knew I was right. Possession was nine-tenths of the law, and they didn't have anything except the Jerk's word versus mine.

One of the officers pushed me down in the chair. "What do these keys go to?" He pointed to the keys hanging from my neck.

"They just old keys that don't work anymore."

As the officer examined the keys closer, he noticed that a couple of them were non-duplicable keys. "Come and take a look at this, Sarge. These non-duplicable keys belong to an apartment building. I'll bet you if we find this place, we find the shit!"

They were right; if they found this place, they would find the shit. I needed to get word out of jail to clean out the apartment, but the cops were smart. They were holding me with no phone calls.

●●●

The cell door opened, and all I could see was this huge cop standing in the doorway.

"You ready to take a ride?"

"Take a ride where?"

Laughing, he said, "You'll see when we get there."

As we pulled onto the interstate, I was dying inside. *Please, Jesus, don't let them have found out where my apartment is. Lord, please get me out of this!* My apartment was in Richmond Heights—if they knew where it was, they would take the next freeway ramp onto 271 North.

Oh shit, they just got on 271 North. Jesus, help me please! If they search this apartment, I will never get out of jail. I stayed silent the entire ride, but my insides were screaming, *HELP.*

When we pulled up to my apartment, the cops abruptly stopped the car and opened my door. "Welcome home, muthafucka."

I sheepishly said, "I don't live here."

They ignored my denial as if I hadn't said a word. *How could they have found this place? The Jerk doesn't know about it.*

Months earlier, I had called the police after an attempted break-in at the apartment. The incident was a matter of police record. They knew about the apartment hours ago and had driven out and tested my keys to ensure they had the right place.

As we arrived at the front door, I nervously repeated, "I don't live here."

"Oh, you don't live here, huh?" He grabbed my keys and unlocked the door. "Why did your keys unlock the door then?" Before I could

Sleeping in the Jungle

answer, he slapped me on the back of the head and said, "Get yo' ass in there."

Although they had me sitting at my own dining room table, the only weapon I had left was to play stupid. "I don't know why you got me in these people's house."

A short black cop I had never seen before sat across the table from me with a sheet of paper. "Sign this consent to search."

"I can't sign for y'all to search somebody else's house."

"You wanna do this the hard way, huh? If you refuse to sign, then write 'refused' so I can get you the fuck out my face."

I took the pen and did as requested, but I wanted to take that pen and stab myself in the neck for putting myself in this situation. *You have to be the dumbest person alive. Why did you trust the Jerk? Where in the hell would he get a thousand dollars? Why didn't you just pass the rest of the dope off for Eaton to sell? Ugh, I hate myself right now!*

My refusal to sign the consent to search had all the officers pissed off at me, because they had to wait several hours for a judge to get out of bed and sign a search warrant. Each hour seemed like a week, and the whole time I was rooting for something to derail this investigation.

Damn, the search warrant's here! Stick a fork in me, this nigga is done. To execute the search warrant, they had to have Richmond Heights Police Department on scene to supervise the search because it was their jurisdiction. All of that for little old me? I had the Cleveland Police Department, the Richmond Heights Police Department, drug-sniffing dogs, helicopters... *Jesus Christ. They act like I'm Pablo Escobar's nephew or something.*

"Ooot oooot ooooot!"

Hell naw! That was not the normal sound a dog made, but I had cooked so much cocaine in this apartment that the dog couldn't pinpoint a location. The drug smell was in the curtains, the carpet, my clothes, everywhere. Uh-oh, the dog was sniffing in the closet where the dope was.

This is it, dammit. Life in prison!

Holy crap, he didn't find it. Every time the dog swung his nose into the closet I thought I was done, but for some reason he was not detecting it. All the drugs were in winter coats. I sewed the coat sleeves closed at the elbow. That way when you put drugs down the sleeve, they stopped halfway down the arm. Unbelievable! The dog didn't find the drugs, but the cops started to conduct a search of their own.

"Guns," one cop yelled. "Tons of ammo."

Every time somebody yelled, I caught a new case. As soon as I had the thought of never getting out of jail, my worst nightmare was realized. One of the cops found the drugs.

The cops celebrated like it was New Year's Eve. "I knew we would get him," one declared. They slapped hands and celebrated the demise of my young life.

Happy Twenty-first

"I'm glad it's over," I whispered at the ceiling of my jail cell. The cops were so pleased with the evidence they gathered that they allowed me to make bail for $2,000. Those cops must've thought I was stupid. The only reason they wanted me on the streets was so they could watch me and, hopefully, I'd lead them to more drugs, or better yet, my supplier. I had a trick for them, though. They could watch me all they wanted, because I was never selling dope again in my life.

The most disheartening thing about catching that case was the cops nearly got all of the hundred grand I had saved up. With no surprise, none of the money made it back to the precinct. The cops said they only found a few hundred bucks in cash. They were the biggest crooks of them all!

Facing a lifetime in jail, nearly broke, and beat up from the ass-whipping the cops gave me, I was about to turn twenty-one in just a few days. *Happy birthday, dumb ass. You can celebrate by finding a good lawyer and slapping the shit out of yourself for not quitting while you were ahead.*

Stanley Vegetarian

Stanley Vegetarian was one of the finest black criminal defense attorneys to ever live. He was my version of Johnnie Cochran. He stood 6'3" tall with a slender build. When he smiled, he made you smile also, but his laugh was the most contagious. Whenever he walked into a room, you knew it because you could hear his loud voice long before you could see him. He was fluent in Spanish and was a champion for the Latino community. He was fluent in sign language and was a champion to the hearing impaired. He was also fluent in ignorance and was a champion to a lot of ignorant people.

Today I was going to him with some ignorant shit. I had a Jerk who turned me in to the cops, and I was facing a decade in jail. Jail was not going to be good for a little man like myself. I'd seen the movies. I had to face the music, and I needed the best lawyer. I was just hoping he would take my case.

"Hello, sir."

"Hey, how are you doing, young man?" he replied like we'd known each other for years. "What brings you into my office today?"

Before I could even muster an answer, my throat got so tight that it was difficult for me to swallow, and tears began to fall. "I messed up big time, sir."

He smiled and said, "You didn't mess up that bad if you're out on bail. It would be different if we were having this conversation while you were in jail wearing an orange jumpsuit. Why don't you tell me what happened?"

While I was running the story down to him, I noticed he was not taking notes. The only thing that seemed to be interesting to him was what they found. I told him it was about sixteen ounces of crack and several firearms. That was the first crack I saw in his armor, and he made a ghastly face as if to say "ouch."

"I know it's bad, sir, but I just want to get this shit over with."

He took off his glasses and looked me in my eyes. "Young man, unfortunately it's going to be a long time before this is over with."

"How much does a case like this cost?"

"It depends on how long the trial goes on. Worse-case scenario is ten thousand, but you can make payments. My retainer is fifteen hundred to start, and once I get the case file from the courts, I will let you know what you're facing. Look, don't worry, I will do my best to minimize the damage."

I paid the $1,500 and cried all the way to the car. Minimize the damage? Man, I was royally screwed! *After I pay him $10,000, I'm going to be broke, Kelli will never speak to me again, and I'm going to go to jail.* I had no family to send me money in jail and no one to write me letters. I wouldn't have anything or anybody. *God, is this why You saved me from being murdered in the house with my father? Just to be another convicted felon with no life? Is this the plan You have for my life? Lord, I know this is my fault, but You know I was about to quit this life. You know I was on the verge of walking away from this drug world. Why did You allow this to happen? Why?*

Stand By Me

One of the first people to track me down to see if I was okay was Kelli. Even with me running from the police in her car, nearly killing us all, and getting her arrested, her main concern was if I was okay. After getting her car out of the impound, she was on her way to come and pick me up.

"Hey, baby," she said as she kissed and held my swollen face.

"Hey, little momma."

"Are you okay?"

"Nah, not really! Look, I'm really sorry about getting you involved in this street shit."

"Don't apologize to me for that. I knew what it was when I signed up. Besides, they let me go with no charges. My car is a little banged up, but that can be fixed."

Totally surprised by her answer, it was difficult to look her in the eye. "Look, it's likely that I'm going to be headed to jail for a long time. You are such a good girl that I don't want to put you in a position of being stuck dealing with a guy like me. So, we should probably go our separate ways bec—"

"No, please don't say that. I got your back. I can help you pay for your lawyer and stand by your side while you're away. Just please don't walk away from me." She gripped my neck in a bear hug.

"Yeah, you say that now, but it's going to be a rough road ahead. We just met a few months ago, and I'm not a fool. Everybody's girl says they are going to stand by them through a prison sentence until they leave. After they're gone, they move on."

She refused to accept my words or release the hold on my neck. "Don't say that! I love you. Give me a chance and I will prove that I'm loyal."

What did I really have to lose? I was broke and soon to be homeless yet again. I had to get my ass in gear and figure out what I was going to do. She said she would be by my side, but only time would tell that. In the meantime, I had to figure out my next steps, but dealing drugs was never going to be an option again!

I was so impressed with Kelli. She was a good girl and would do anything to help me. She put a down payment on a new house so we could have a place to live together. True to her word, she was standing by her man. She attended all my court hearings with me and even helped me with the payments I made to Stanley. We had only known each other for six months, and I saw more love and loyalty than I'd ever felt from anyone in my entire life. What would I ever do without her?

Although she'd been by my side throughout my case, I believed things would change drastically when I was locked up. Once I was gone, every man in the world was going to be after a beautiful girl who had a great job, owned her own home, and didn't have any children. I would do anything to be able to stay with my beloved Kelli, but that was not going to be possible. I would see how much she loved me when I had to spend years in prison. These were the bad times. You had to have buzzard luck to meet the perfect girl after you'd already screwed your life up.

An Angel Can Change Things

"I can't believe you have thrown your entire life away. Was it worth it? Look at your dumb ass now. Say something." Unfortunately, the mirror in the bathroom of the Justice Center couldn't talk back. I had to take my ass back out there and sit by the courtroom and await my punishment like a man. The seats outside the courtroom looked as if they had comfortable cushions on them, but after two hours of sitting down, my ass was about to explode. Finally, I saw my attorney step off the elevator so we could get the show on the road.

"What's up, Stanley?" I greeted him as I tried to mask my nervousness.

Sleeping in the Jungle

"Everything's all right, young man. Don't worry about today. It's just a formality. We are going to file a motion to suppress the evidence because I found some discrepancies in the officers' account of what happened. It's a Hail Mary, but we will see what the judge says."

"I know you got it, but I sure hope they know they have a good man out here."

"Ha ha ha, I hear that. Have a seat and I will be back out shortly."

•••

"Hello, ma'am," I said to a woman sitting in African garb as I took a seat.

"Hello, my son."

After thirty minutes of sitting and waiting, the worry was taking over my entire body. Out of the blue, the lady reached out her hand and said, "My name is Queen Mother."

"Hello, my name is David King."

"David, I can see that you are troubled. Are you expecting bad news?"

"There's always some bad news happening down here. I'm in a lot of trouble, but I'm hoping for the best."

"Life is hard, young man. There's plenty of opportunity to end right back up in this building, even if you were to catch a break."

"That's true, but I have truly changed my ways. I know this lifestyle is not for me, but I have dug a hole too large to get out of at this point. The only thing I can do is hope for the best outcome and try to salvage the rest of my life."

I had been talking to this woman for a while and I never really got a good look at her. She was a short lady, about 5'6", and extremely dark-skinned. Her head and body were dressed in African garb but she also had on a lot of rhinestone jewelry. She was speaking to me sternly and was purposeful in her questioning, but there was something about her that was compelling me to keep answering.

"David, what would you do with a second chance?"

"Ma'am—"

"Queen Mother."

"I mean, Queen Mother, I would live my life right. I will change my life for the better and help other people in my situation."

Unexpectedly she became emotional as she whispered, "I believe you, son. I believe you."

Just as we concluded our conversation, a sheriff came out of an adjacent courtroom with a prisoner dressed in orange. This was odd, because when prisoners had court, they were brought up through a back elevator, but for some reason the sheriff was walking the guy through the sitting area. As the prisoner was being walked across the walkway, he turned and nodded at Queen Mother. She nodded back at him, and the sheriff and prisoner entered the courtroom where Stanley had entered almost an hour earlier.

"Was that who you are visiting for court?" I asked Queen Mother, but for some strange reason, she didn't reply. I was getting up the nerve to ask again when the doors to the courtroom burst open.

Stanley was waving his arms and swinging papers in excitement. "We got it, we got it!" He pulled me into a side room. "The judge granted our motion to suppress."

"What the hell does that mean?"

"This means the judge just deemed all of the evidence against you inadmissible."

"Speak fucking English, Stanley."

"In other words, the prosecution has to drop any charges for what they found in your apartment. They can only prosecute you for the car chase."

I can't believe it! As we left the room, I went into the bathroom to call everyone I knew. Exiting the bathroom, I glanced around the courtroom waiting area and the only person I saw was Queen Mother.

"It looks like you got a favorable outcome! Was that the break you needed?"

"Absolutely."

"I believe you were sincere when you said you will turn your life around, my son."

"I am and I will! Thank you so much for the encouragement and positive words. I really needed that."

Rising to her feet, she only muttered a few words. "Thank me by living your life a faithful young man. Faithful. Your destiny is too great."

The Unexpected After the Unexpected

Just as Stanley said, the case was dropped. The motion to suppress the evidence was granted because when the Cleveland Police drove me out to my apartment, they used my keys to open the door without Richmond Heights Police being present at the time of entering. All the evidence was considered tainted. The day they drove to my home and sat me at my own dining room table was the only reason why I escaped prison and gained an opportunity to live again. I was not out of the woods yet, though. There was still the matter of fleeing and eluding the police and hitting a police car. In addition, there was a small case of possession of criminal tools found in the car at the time of my arrest. The fleeing and eluding charge was a felony in the fourth degree, and the possession case was a felony in the fifth degree. The prosecution was offering a deal. If I pled guilty to the felony five possession, they would drop the felony four fleeing and eluding. A guilty plea carried a maximum of twelve months in jail and a minimum of probation.

"I'll take it, Stanley." We shook hands in the hallway. "I can never thank you enough."

Although I beat these charges, it seemed like there was something very different in the attitude of my judge. He was the one who granted the motion to suppress the evidence, but for some reason, he seemed angry with me. "Mr. King, please stand for sentencing."

Rising to my feet, I felt an overwhelming sense of confidence because I had a lot of positive things going for me. I was in college. I was a clean-cut kid who had never been in prison before. I knew I was going to get probation. A felony five wasn't shit. It was the cops' fault that they bungled the case. I deserved to go home.

The judge's voice boomed through the room. "Mr. King, are you satisfied with your lawyer?"

"Yes I am, your honor."

"You should be." With a slight smile, the judge looked me directly in my eyes as if he could see the confidence beaming through my veins. "Mr. King, if I sentence you to the maximum sentence of twelve months, you and your attorney will appeal and you will get a new judge who will not see any of the evidence that was presented against you in this case. All he would see is this minor felony. Mr. King, I have no doubt that this judge will allow you to remain free on probation. It is my belief that by setting you free, you may go back to the same lifestyle you've been living. You are a criminal, Mr. King, and you are going to prison. I hereby sentence you to eleven months in the Ohio Department of Corrections. One month under the maximum so you can't appeal. Don't send me any paperwork about early release or shock probation once you get to prison either. You will do every minute of this eleven months."

Wham! The gavel slammed against the bench.

"Bailiff, take him away!"

My eyes widened to the size of bowling balls. That didn't go anything like I expected. I turned and gave Stanley a desperate look, but there was nothing he could do. I turned to look at Kelli with my eyes filled with worry as the bailiff put me in handcuffs and began to escort me away.

"No!" Kelli screamed. Looking at her crying in agony, I couldn't help thinking that this was the last time I was going to see her as my girlfriend. Nobody waited for a guy in jail. *Shit, I'm the one who should be crying.*

Changing into my bright orange jumpsuit, I couldn't help feeling extreme fright about the road ahead. I had never been to prison before. What the hell was my dumb ass going to do around real criminals? I couldn't believe I was going to jail. I'd been celebrating for the past two months thinking I'd beaten the case and was planning for the future. I was so sure I was walking free that I had dinner reservations for the next day.

Thinking Ahead

Every level in the county jail had pods. The pod consisted of two tiers. Twenty-five jail cells on the top tier and twenty-five on the bottom. The floor was covered with about fifteen tables made of steel and bolted to the floor. There were forty to fifty men standing around everywhere, and in front of all that chaos stood a guard's desk. There was only one guard for all of us inmates because they didn't need more. That one guard was one button away from summoning twenty of the largest, meanest officers in the world if some trouble arose. They called them the Goon Squad.

I was finally in my cell. That was a crazy-ass day. My living quarters consisted of a two-by-eight concrete slab with a skinny three-inch mat and a nappy wool cover. There was a crusty-looking black dude lying on one side of the cell snuggled under a blanket that barely covered his body. The cell had an overwhelming foot odor. It smelled like the kind of feet you'd have after you played twenty-six games of basketball in one-hundred-degree weather. This guy must have been in the cell a long time, because he didn't even turn around to see who was coming in. I didn't expect the guy to roll out the red carpet, but he should want to see what somebody looked like who was moving into his cell. If he was sleeping on the concrete slab, I guess that meant I was sleeping on the floor. *Oh no, I have to put my mat on the floor next to the toilet that's in the corner. Lord, take me now!*

•••

The doors shook. "Breakfast," the officer yelled.

Shit. I'd slept from the moment I'd lain down until morning? It had to be extreme exhaustion. The intensity of the day before had left me in shambles.

Although I was absolutely flabbergasted that I was in jail, it wasn't a total surprise. I was thinking ahead in the event that if I did get locked up, I needed a plan. There were a lot of criminals who told me if you were sentenced to prison time, you usually stayed in the county jail for about seven days before you rode out to prison. That seven days was hard, because you didn't have time to get money on your account so you could go to the store for goodies. My intelligence would not allow me to sit in jail and rely completely on jail food, so I'd stashed a small sack of marijuana in my ass just in case I had to do a short stint.

I could get ten bags of chips or cookies for one small joint. Once the guys on the pod found out that I had the weed, I was the most popular guy in jail. I wasn't passing out one joint until all the weed was sold. I knew that once the guard smelled it the first time, our entire pod was going to get shaken down by the Goon Squad, and I didn't want any of it to be left over.

Sleeping in the Jungle

Ten joints and a hundred goodies later, my cell was loaded.

"Now we can smoke, but where are we going to smoke at?" I asked a few of the other inmates.

Before I could finish getting the words out, this real ugly dude blurted out, "Y'all can smoke in my cell if you let me smoke with you." Dummy! When we got shaken down, he was going to the hole for sure.

"Let's do it! I could only sneak one match in the bag with my sack of weed, so we have to make it count." *Chick-chick-poof.* The match was lit. "Hurry up. Y'all get y'all's lit."

After just a few hits I was good and passed mine to the ugly freeloader. "This smell is out of control. I'm leaving y'all." I hurried down the stairs to my cell while they were still smoking. I had to quickly grab a towel and shower shoes. If I got in the shower before the pod got raided, I could get the weed smell off me and escape going to the hole.

Come on, shower water, get warm so I can get in. Come on, come on, dammit. "Oh shit, the alarms." *Please hurry and get wet. The Goon Squad is coming—fuck!*

"LOCKDOWN, LOCKDOWN. GET THE FUCK ON THE GROUND NOW."

With nothing but soap on my hands and chest, I yelled, "I'M IN THE SHOWER."

"GET THE FUCK OUT HERE NOW. NOW, MOTHERFUCKER."

I dove out of the shower naked and soapy and lay on the floor. I looked around and saw a sea of other inmates face down on the floor as well.

"WHO GOT THE MOTHERFUCKIN' WEED?" a man in all black demanded.

Silence…

"OKAY, Y'ALL WANT TO FUCK WITH ME? EVERYBODY LINE UP AGAINST THE WALL. I'M SMELLING YOUR FINGERS. IF

Elle B. Six

ANYBODY'S FINGERS SMELL LIKE WEED, YOU'RE GOING TO THE HOLE AND YOU'RE GETTING HIT WITH MORE CHARGES."

My criminal compadres hadn't planned for this, but I had. I knew their guilty fingers would get them busted. Their hands smelled like weed and mine smelled like soap! I was hoping I'd gotten all the smell off me, but the guards didn't even sniff me because I'd been in the shower and therefore they assumed I couldn't have been involved. *Damn, I'm good!* Like dominoes, they fell one after another. All nine guys were heading to the hole, and I got to finish my shower. Just the way I planned it.

"EVERYBODY IN THIS POD IS LOCKED DOWN FOR THIRTY DAYS," the sergeant yelled as he was leaving. Everyone was grumbling except for me. I was high, I wasn't in the hole, I was riding out to prison in six days, and I had a hundred cakes and pies in my cell. What was there to grumble about?

The Ride

Boom, click, click—the cell door opened.

The guard said, "KING?"

"Yeah."

"What's your date of birth?"

"June 29th, 1976."

"Pack your stuff, you're riding out!"

All I could think was, *This is it. Prison. What in the world have you gotten yourself into? Lord, I need You on this one.* I packed my two bags of bullshit before making my way to the waiting bus. I couldn't believe it, but this walk was just like in the movies. I was dressed in all orange and shackled at the wrist and ankle to a stinky-ass old dude. I had to be shackled to this guy for a five-hour bus ride, and he smelled like six different kinds of ass. If the Lord was trying to make things as uncomfortable as possible so I would get my life together, it was working.

Thank you, Lord! I finally saw the Lorain Correctional facility in the distance. I went from being afraid of going to the prison to happy, because I was dying being shackled to this old funky fucker. By the fifth hour, his ass smell had finally burned through my nasal cavity and penetrated my tear ducts. I looked like I was crying, and he kept leaning over, saying in his monotone deep voice, "It's cool, little bruh. You gon' be all right. Prison ain't shit. You ain't got nothing to worry about."

I wanted to tell this dude so badly to please stop leaning over to talk. All that rocking back and forth had to be what was heating that ass smell up.

As we approached the prison, I squinted my eyes to sharpen my vision through my tears. *What a monster!* Five layers of fence laced with razor wire. There were twenty or thirty brown and green buildings and hundreds of thousands of square feet to hold society's worst. I had finally made it to the place I feared most. I couldn't help feeling that I deserved this. I couldn't have feared it that much if I'd committed as many crimes as I had. I needed to just suck it up and do what I had to do to get back to my family. However, my first priority was getting the hell off this bus and separating from this ass smell. I hoped I never had to see this guy ever again in my life!

"KING," an officer yelled at the top of his lungs.

"Yes, sir."

"Come here. Take your clothes off."

I walked over and complied as if this behavior was normal, but my heart was about to jump out of my chest. As I stood there naked, the corrections officer began asking me a series of stupid-ass questions like, "Do you have any identifying tattoos?"

I thought, *Muthafucka, I'm asshole naked. What damn tattoos do you see?*

Once the questions turned serious and he asked me if I was trying to smuggle anything into the prison, I knew the questions were over and the orders would begin. The order you knew was coming but dreaded the most.

"Lift up your nut sack. Bend over and spread your ass cheeks. Wider. Now cough."

I had never been so humiliated in my life. Having to do that in front of about fifty different people instantly deflated my ability to be shocked by anything I saw there. This was about to be some bullshit.

The Odd Inmates

I was assigned to a two-man cell; I didn't have to be housed on the floor where there were about a hundred bunk beds. There were a hundred cells that surrounded the beds that were out there on the floor. After dark, anything went down on the floor. Just as I gained comfort in being in a two-man cell, I got nervous thinking about the guy on the bus. What if my cellmate was a stinky-ass dude? Or even worse, what if my cellmate was the dude from the bus? We got checked in one behind the other. Did they assign cells in the order you came in? *Help.*

What a relief. My cellmate was not a stinky guy. In fact, he was surprisingly normal. Normal from a personal perspective, but completely abnormal in thinking. He was a middle-aged white guy with all the hair missing from the middle of his head. He wore big brown-tinted bifocals and sported a bushy mustache. After completing a nine-year sentence for attempted murder, he'd only been out of jail for twenty-four hours before he'd caught a new case. On his new case, he

Sleeping in the Jungle

was serving a twenty-two-year sentence. How the hell did they have me in there with a guy doing twenty-two years and I only had eleven months? I had been in some scary situations in my life, and the only way to remedy a scary situation was through laughter. So I had to do what I knew best.

"What's your name again, my friend?"

"Donald."

"Okay, Donald, let me get this straight. You served nine years in prison, and were out twenty-four hours before getting another twenty-two years?"

"YUP."

"You got to be the stupidest muthafucka I have ever met in my entire life."

He erupted with laughter.

"Did this twenty-two-year crime involve some sex?"

"No, the time is for aggravated robbery."

"You didn't even have time to get some pussy. Don't let me catch you sliding off that top bunk with no gleam in your eye, or I'm gon' shorten that sentence up for you real fast."

He was doubled over from laughter, so I couldn't stop.

"As a matter of fact, I'm about to go to sleep. I don't even want to talk to you no more. Take yo no-pussy-gettin' ass to sleep too."

We laughed our way to sleep, and a friendship began.

I nicknamed Donald "24" since his dumb ass had only been free for twenty-four hours before returning to jail. He nicknamed me "Shorty" because of my height, no doubt. Once Donald finally got around to telling me what he did to get twenty-two years, I really wasn't prepared for what he said. When he'd finally gotten out from doing nine years, his family had been so happy. They'd bought him a car to drive, and he'd spent the entire day celebrating. His family owned some land that had a huge lake with a canoe for boating. He and a lifelong friend had gone to the liquor store and had been out on the canoe drinking all night. They'd been so drunk that they'd kept capsizing the boat. One of the times the boat had capsized, the edge of the boat had sliced his shin open. The cut was so nasty that they'd decided to head back to the shore to treat the wound. After the wound had been patched by two of the drunkest assholes on the planet, he and his friend had gone their separate ways.

Drunk, bleeding profusely from the leg, and fresh out of jail, he'd really needed some money so he could continue to party. He'd remembered a scam he used to run on the Amish farmers who purchased farm equipment from a nearby auction.

He told me the Amish didn't believe in banks, so they always carried cash. After spotting a horse and carriage coming from the auction, he would park his car on the side of the road with the hood up. When the Amish buggy would stop to help him, he would rob them of their cash.

Once he spotted the buggy he wanted to rob, he parked his car, and sure enough, the buggy had stopped to help. Then he'd pulled a knife on the guy and had walked him back to the buggy where the Amish man's wife was holding the cash. Donald had ordered the woman out of the buggy. When she'd gotten out, the Amish man told her to give him the money. When the Amish lady refused, Donald sucker punched her.

"Damn, 24, why did you punch her?"

"I was drunk, and I didn't have time for dumb shit. This was a robbery. You can't be no polite robber. You have to let them know you mean business."

He went on to say that he wished he hadn't hit her, because once he'd landed the blow to the wife, the husband had rushed over and tackled him. He'd beaten them both up and made off with the money.

"Shorty, this is very important, because it really speaks to how drunk I was. As I made off with the money from my robbery, I spotted another Amish buggy and tried to do the same shit again."

"You tried to rob another buggy?"

"Hell yeah with my dumb ass. The first Amish couple made it to call for help and gave them my description. I was in the middle of robbing the second buggy when the police came flying down the street and arrested me. The funny thing is, when we got to court, the lady I punched didn't even recognize me. The reason I got convicted was after I punched her and the husband tackled me, some of the blood from my busted shin got on his shirt. When they ran the DNA, it was a perfect match, and off to prison I went."

"24, why did you try to do it again after you had gotten away with the money the first time?"

"I have no idea." For the first time, I could see him on the edge of emotion as his eyes filled with tears.

"Hey, 24…did I forget to tell you that you got to be the stupidest muthafucka I ever met in my life?"

He burst out laughing.

"No wonder they sent yo' ass to jail. You don't deserve to walk among civilized people. All they gave yo' ass is twenty-two years? Shit, you lucky I wasn't on that jury. I woulda gave your ass the death penalty for being so damn dumb."

We laughed our way to sleep.

Camp Reams

My cellmate was a real sociopath. I was kidding with him, but this guy was truly a danger to society and should have been locked away for life. My only sanity was reading the letters from my angel Kelli. My angel sent from heaven who wrote me letters every day. If there was a day that I didn't get a letter, there must have been a holdup at the post office, because the next day I would get two letters. Where would I be without her? I had always been taught by my dad that you couldn't trust a woman because a woman didn't have the ability to love anyone but herself. That couldn't be true, because I was in prison and she had the ability to be free. Instead of running around on me, she was spending every day of her freedom professing her love through letters. I loved to write her back on occasion, but I didn't write as much as she did. I spent most of my time worrying and reading books.

I began talking to a corrections officer named Kenny. Kenny was cool. He told me about a place called Camp Reams, a military-style boot camp for first-time prisoners. If you completed the program, you could go home in ninety days. All I could hear in the back of my mind was my judge saying, "*Don't even try to get out early.*"

When I told the corrections officer what my judge said, he said, "What are the odds he will remember you? He has a thousand of these requests coming into his office daily, and he was probably not even the one approving them. The worst thing he can say is no, right?"

I needed something to hang my hat on. I needed some hope that I wouldn't spend eleven months of my life in this hell hole. I went for it, because I had to get back home. I sent in my request to the Bureau of Prisons and let fate take its course. *Lord, please let me get back so I don't lose her.*

I got my answer from the Bureau of Prisons and I could hardly believe it. It got approved. *Holy shit, I got it!*

"Officer Kenny, I got it, my brother. I can't thank you enough for tipping me off about Camp Reams. I'm going home!"

"Congratulations, young man. Just make sure you don't end up back here again. You seem like a very conscientious person, not like many of the guys I see come through here. You got a good head on your shoulders. Don't waste it."

"I won't, sir. I won't."

It wasn't long before I began to worry about Camp Reams. I never really thought I was going to get approved to go. The only thing I'd considered was going home in ninety days. The more I asked around, the more nervous I got. The key to going home in ninety days was that you had to complete the program. The military-style requirements might be too much for me because I was completely out of shape. I was 5'5" but I weighed 212 pounds. Rumor had it that you had to run ten miles a day. I couldn't run one mile in a day. Somehow I had to make it, because it was the only way I was going to claim my freedom. I had to make it.

•••

This was my last day in the prison before I headed to Camp Reams. I was nervous as hell.

The doors to the cell unlocked. Officer Kenny ducked his head in and asked, "Are you guys taking showers tonight?"

Simultaneously 24 and I both said yes.

"Okay, you first," he instructed, pointing to 24. Once 24 left the cell, Kenny returned to my cell. This was highly unusual, because protocol was for the guard to return with the inmate before taking me down to the shower area. After Kenny walked in, he looked around and dropped something on my bed.

"What is this, sir?" As I picked up what he dropped, I noticed it was a burger. "Holy shit, is this what I think it is?" *Hell yeah…a quarter pounder with cheese.*

"Listen, young man. You're leaving here tomorrow. If anyone catches you with that burger, you are going to the hole, and I'm going to lose my job. The best thing you can do is make sure there isn't a trace of it left. Good luck with your future, and don't let me catch you back here again."

"Wow, than' roo, sir, than' roo." I was barely able to speak, because half the burger was stuffed in my mouth.

As Officer Kenny left, I couldn't help thinking that this was the greatest-tasting burger I'd ever eaten. Had Mickey D's always tasted this exquisite? Just as I devoured the last bite, I felt a tingling in my pants. *Oh my God, what the hell is that?* I ran over to the small sink in my cell. I pulled down my pants, and to my amazement, my dick was rock hard. I couldn't believe it. *Did I just get a hard-on from a quarter pounder with cheese?* I could never tell anybody that shit. I'll bet they won't advertise that in a commercial. Good looking out, Mickey D's!

● ● ●

Camp Reams was in Lancaster, Ohio. It had its own separate facility but it shared fences with the notorious Lancaster State Prison. Lancaster Prison looked like every haunted house you'd ever seen. Tall, dark-brown buildings surrounded by fences and razor wire. Hundreds of prisoners walking inside each gate. This was not what I expected. This place looked more menacing than the place I'd just left. There must've been a mistake. This place housed society's worst. It couldn't be the place where people went home in ninety days.

To my relief, after passing a dozen buildings, we pulled up to a small fenced-in property that looked to be no more than 15,000 square feet. There were guys running around in uniforms exercising and yelling chants while marching. This was more like it. Whatever it took to get me back home, I had to do it. Besides, when I got out, at least I would be in shape.

The first week I spent in the camp was called the ghost period. During the ghost period, I didn't do anything but watch how the camp

Sleeping in the Jungle

was run. I watched how people talked and interacted with drill instructors and observed the day-to-day requirements. After that, I could decide if I wanted to go forward with the program or go back to prison to finish my full sentence. I saw that it was going to be hard, but I was going for it.

Day one of the actual program had arrived, and I thought I was going to lose my mind because they woke us up at 4:59 a.m. There were so many people yelling that I didn't know what the hell was going on.

The drill instructor was yelling at the same time he was cutting my hair. "YOU'RE A PIECE OF SHIT! Don't look at me with your stinking FUCKING EYEBALLS. Look down!"

"Yes, sir."

"IT'S NOT 'YES, SIR,' ASSHOLE. IT'S 'SIR, YES SIR.'"

"Sir, yes sir."

"I CAN'T HEAR YOU. GET ON THE GROUND AND GIVE ME TWENTY-FIVE PUSH-UPS."

I fell to the ground on my belly and I couldn't help thinking, *What the hell did I get myself into?*

"COUNT 'EM OUT, PRISONER. TWENTY-FIVE PUSH-UPS. LET'S GO."

Pushing up, I said, "One, sir."

"IT'S NOT 'ONE, SIR,' IT'S 'SIR, ONE SIR.' I SEE NOW YOU'RE NOT GOING TO MAKE IT, FAT BODY. YOU CAN'T EVEN DO TWENTY-FIVE PUSH-UPS. YOU WANT TO GO UP TO THE PRISON TO SUCK SOME DICKS, DON'T YOU? WHY DON'T YOU JUST QUIT NOW."

"SIR, NO SIR!"

"OOOOOH, WE GOT A KEEPER, HUH? WELL WE WILL SEE HOW LONG THAT LASTS. I'M GOING TO SEE TO IT THAT YOU QUIT, FAT BODY. YOU'LL SEE!"

This was only the end of day one, and I couldn't feel anything but pain. My body was so tired that I couldn't move. I was lying in my room with five other guys on small cots. *Oh my God, how am I going to get back to Kelli if I can't finish this program?* I had the drive, but it was not physically possible for me to complete these exercises every day. As my eyes welled up with tears, I felt completely helpless. *Please, God, help me. I'm so sore, Lord, but I need You to help me make it through this please.*

"Please," I whispered as I cried myself to sleep.

When day two arrived, I knew there was no way I could make it through another round of physical torture. After I jumped out of my bed and stood at attention to await the morning instruction from the drill instructors, I noticed something missing. The pain! Where had the soreness gone? Last night I could hardly move, but today I felt completely normal. How in the world could this be?

We ran two miles on day two, and the night before I couldn't walk. I couldn't explain it, but I was so glad it happened.

My body was adapting to the new environment better than I could ever imagine. I felt myself getting stronger and stronger as the days progressed. I felt my mind getting stronger as the drill instructors instilled discipline, honor, and responsibility into my life. By day forty-five, I was a squared-away model prisoner.

My reason for pushing through the torture was Kelli. I was almost home, and she still hadn't missed one day of writing me. That was truly an amazing feat. I didn't think it was possible for anyone to love me the way she did. I wanted to marry her and spend the rest of my life with her. I had no idea if she would accept my hand in marriage, but I had to make an honest woman of her. After I got out of here, I had two missions—get a job, and make her my wife.

Halfway Home

Camp Reams was having a significant impact on my thinking! I was not sure what the other prisoners were learning from the experience, but I was experiencing discipline in every area of my life. The importance of exercise, respect, hard work, honor, integrity, education, and perseverance. When I'd arrived at the camp, I'd been required to run a mile in under eight minutes. I'd run it in seventeen minutes. I'd thought it was impossible for me to run it under eight. By day seventy-five, I could run the mile in seven minutes flat. You could train your body when to be hungry, when to use the bathroom, and when to rest. At Camp Reams, they taught me to eliminate the word "CAN'T" from my vocabulary.

Because of my college background, I had the opportunity to tutor other prisoners who were studying for their GED. Teaching grown men fundamentals of education helped me to realize just how blessed I was. The more I taught them, the more I developed techniques to help them learn faster. There were men who told me that out of all the years they tried to study for their GED, I was the first teacher who made sense. I helped eight guys get their GED, and they all told me they would never forget me for helping them.

I put everything I had into becoming the best prisoner to come through the camp. My standout ability landed me a job cleaning up the facility at night by myself. Buffing floors, cleaning offices, showers, and so on. Even though it was hard work, the job had its rewards. Every week when there were new prisoners arriving at the camp, the drill instructors threw all the food they brought with them into a big dumpster outside. Just after midnight, when all the prisoners were asleep, the night guard would let me dive into the dumpster and pull out any goodies that I wanted. I never thought I could be so happy diving into a trash dumpster to get food, but there were dozens of unopened cookies, candy bars, and potato chips. Mondays were pig-out days, and no one had any idea. I was coasting my way home.

Finally, it was time to leave Camp Reams. I did my ninety days in the camp, and the only thing left between me and freedom was a brief stay at a halfway house. After thirty days in the halfway house, I was on my way home.

Although I was afraid of what the world had to offer me when I got back, I was also optimistic. I knew I would never do anything illegal again. My heart and my mind had been made anew. I was grateful for the lessons the Lord had taught me, and I was ready to rebuild my life in His image. *Get ready, world, here comes the new me.*

The New Block

On May 13, 2000, I was freed and no longer the property of the State of Ohio. Kelli was waiting outside the doors with her face filled with tears. We hugged for what seemed like an hour. The ride home, all we could talk about was the future. I couldn't believe that she'd waited for me. We had only known each other six months before I'd gotten arrested and only a year before I'd gone to prison. She had stuck with me as if we were lifelong partners, and that was something that I would never forget. Only God could have sent her from heaven, because she was the only family that I had.

Fresh out of jail, my number-one priority was to get a job so I could provide for my daughter and make an honest woman out of my beloved Kelli. There was no way I could ask her to marry me without having a job. Although I was a street hustler who'd made hundreds of thousands of dollars, the one thing I didn't have was pride. I would work anywhere for any wage just as long as it was honest. I was a young twenty-one-year-old man in fantastic shape, easy on the eyes, and articulate. There had to be an employer looking for someone like me, right? Wrong! Application after application, there was no work for drug dealers fresh out of jail. I knew shit was bad when Mickey D's didn't even want me. I didn't know what I was going to do, but I knew I had to do something.

There was very little interest in hiring convicted felons. The only saving grace that I could hang my hat on was the application I put in at the job of Kelli's brother-in-law. He worked in a steel manufacturing company called Steel Shot. The job would be perfect for me.

I answered no to the portion of the application that asked if you had been convicted of a felony. I was tired of the embarrassment and feeling let down from losing job opportunities because of my criminal past. It was worth a shot.

Hell yeah, I got hired on the spot! I guess it was true what they say: *"It's not what you know, it's who you know."* Kelli's brother-in-law's name was Mack, and he was the man around there. He'd been at Steel Shot for more than ten years and was the only African American machine operator in the whole company. His muscular frame and dark-brown skin usually left people who didn't know him intimidated, but at Steel Shot, he was beloved by everyone.

Although you saw multi-million-dollar machinery running with ease, it wasn't wise to get too comfortable. Everything in that place could kill you. The hundred-thousand-square-foot facility was filled to the rafters with steel coils ranging from ten to forty thousand pounds. If something fell on you, you would be flatter than a pancake. If you rubbed up against the side of something, you would get cut down to the bone. I didn't know if I was more afraid of getting hurt or someone finding out about my past. Either way, I had to watch my ass.

Although it was my first job and I'd only been there for two months, I was quickly learning the political hierarchy of things. There were packagers like me, shipper/receivers, machine operators, then supervisors. Each level higher was less labor intensive but made more money. Now that I knew my position got paid the least but did the most work, I had to angle myself for the top spot. How on earth could I do that when I was the new guy and there were ninety other employees in front of me? Some of them had more than twenty years of experience. Not to mention Mack was the only black guy to break the glass ceiling of becoming a machine operator. If there was a way, I would find it. I had to.

●●●

After one year on the job, I was still in the same place as when I'd gotten there. There was not a single person there hungrier than me. They also didn't know that over the past year, I'd been planning my next moves. Whenever business was slow, I went over to Mack's station and asked questions. I took meticulous notes. "What does this button do? How do you do this? How do you do that?" The only labor-intensive job a machine operator did was set up knives. "Yo, Mack. Teach me how to set those knives up, and I can knock it out for you while you do your paperwork."

No one would turn down that deal. It made the cushiest job of being a machine operator even easier when you got someone to do your knife setups for you. The other guys hated me because they thought I was brown-nosing, but they didn't understand it was all part of the plan.

I had two theories. First, the more I knew, the less likely they would want to fire me if they found out my past. Second, although Mack was the only black machine operator, if a machine operator position became available, why would they waste their time training an operator when I already knew how to do it? Whenever Mack was on vacation, his machine usually had to shut down. Now that I knew how to run the machine, I volunteered to run it in Mack's absence. I did so for no additional pay, and I ran it just as well as Mack. The bosses up front saw my worth, and they were very impressed.

Having a job was just like selling dope on the block. There were ten guys selling rocks just like you, but there had to be a way for you to stand out to make money. In one year, I'd taken over the block and had been getting more money than everybody else. At Steel Shot, there were ninety people in front of me to get promoted, but in one year I was promoted to machine operator and making more money than them all. It was better money, but I noticed that the sweetest job in the entire place was the supervisor position. He just sat in his office until he decided to walk around to make sure we were all working. He didn't lift a finger, but he made more than all of us. Earning a machine operator position was one thing, but a supervisor position was what I had my mind fixed on. *Nothing is impossible when you have the favor of God!*

Trying My Best

I noticed the one weakness in the competition at Steel Shot was that there was no one with a college education, so I decided it was time to continue my education again. I was enrolled once before, but a small obstacle called prison got in the way. It was easy to get back into the groove, but going to school full time and working full time left little time for a personal life. I had spent very little time with my daughter since being released, and she was growing up fast. Laura was seven years old now, and she had developed a very sharp view of the world around her. Her mom had given birth to another daughter and had gotten married shortly after her birthday. Whenever I called Laura, she was very short on the phone and even angrier with me when I picked her up. She was giving her mom and new stepdad hell as well. I paid child support for her and tried to spoil her any chance I got, but there was no substitute for having me physically there. She saw her stepdad dot-

SLEEPING IN THE JUNGLE

ing on his daughter, feeding her, bathing her, and doing fatherly things, which I believe was the source of her bitterness at us all. She felt as if she was cheated out of that. I prayed that one day she would grow older and see that we were doing the best we could, but that was going to take some time. She disliked everyone, but she hated me.

I Do

Mack and Kelli's sister, Kim, were celebrating their twentieth wedding anniversary aboard a huge boat called the *Nautica*. It was the perfect night to be out on the waters of Lake Erie. The waves were calm, and the breeze was just right. As the boat got farther away from land, you could see the shimmer of the Cleveland city lights in the distance. Although we toasted the special marital milestone of Mack and Kim, I felt the overwhelming urge to make this night a milestone myself. I was amazed at how beautiful Kelli looked in her white silky dress flowing in the wind, and before you knew it, I was on my knee. That was the moment, and this was the place. I didn't even have a ring, but it still felt right. When I looked up from my knee and saw the tears well up in Kelli's eyes, I knew I would spend the rest of my life with this woman. "I know I don't have a ring, but one day I will put a ring on your finger larger than this boat. Will you make me the happiest man in the world and marry me?"

Unable to fight back the tears anymore, she said, "Of course I will marry you, and I don't care if I ever have a ring."

I rose to my feet to a huge embrace, a huge kiss, and a huge round of applause. I heard the people clapping but I didn't see them. There was nobody on that boat but Kelli and me.

•••

Love of my life

Our wedding day began rainy, but just before we walked into Maple Heights City Hall, the sun shone as bright as ever. We got married with nobody around but the two of us and two court-appointed witnesses. Kelli and I were going to conquer the world together. On September 14th, 2000, we made the vow before God that we would become one, and I took my queen home for the first time as Mr. and Mrs. KING.

Patience

Kelli and I were watching a documentary about Africa. There was an African tribe that was living in the bush. They had very few possessions, but the one thing they had that stuck out most was a small puppy named Patience with angelic eyes. He had black fur on most of his body, but there were small patches of light brown on his back and head.

He was adorable. Everyone in the village loved Patience, especially the children. The villagers took Patience wherever they went. When you saw them coming, Patience would be trotting right along beside them. Everyone pitched in to care for the little guy. They didn't have much food, so the villagers would all share in the feeding of their faithful pooch. Over the next couple of years, Patience was like one of the family. He had grown into a medium-sized dog by then, and he loved every member of the village equally. On Patience's third birthday, the story began to take a twist. The narrator made a horrific proclamation that on the third birthday of any village animal, the animal was to be sacrificed. I stopped to make sure I'd heard him correctly as my wife let out a ghastly sound. "Oh my God!"

Not only was it tradition to sacrifice little Patience, but it was tradition that every member of the village would participate in the killing. We watched in pure disbelief as the members of the tribe surrounded their trusting friend and took turns beating him until he expired. The look of pure terror and disbelief was on the poor guy's face as he ran to other members of the tribe to escape, only to be met by another blow. The end finally came, and little Patience took his last breath. Killed by the hands of the very people he'd served, loved, and given so much joy. Once he was dead, the villagers had to take the sacrifice, cook it, and have a meal.

I had never seen anything on TV that broke my heart this way. My wife and I cried, held each other, and promised we were going to get a dog and give him the best life that any dog ever had. We were going to spoil him rotten. There was only one name that would be suitable for our new pampered pooch. His name was going to be Patience.

I began searching the newspaper for a new puppy for Kelli and me. We had always been in love with the Pomeranian breed because they were so small and adorable. The only problem was they were extremely expensive. Everywhere I looked, I saw prices of $900, $1,500, and

some breeders were charging as much as $3,000. With all the outrageous prices out there, I found one breeder who said she had a white Pomeranian for only $300. He'd just been born but she needed room in her kennel for a fresh litter.

The moment we saw this adorable pooch, we thought there had to be a catch. He was a purebred and six weeks old. We purchased him and drove him straight to the vet. Once we arrived, it became clear why the breeder had sold him so cheap. He had a bad heart murmur. We didn't care what ailments he had—we would get him the treatment he needed in honor of the African Patience who'd lost his life.

Born September 5th, 2005, this two-pound, five-ounce bundle of joy had all white fur and was barely able to fit in the palm of my hand. It was a family decision that we didn't want to have any children, so this was our child. He stole my wife's heart the moment they locked eyes. We had a renewed purpose in our lives making sure the new Patience had a life the original Patience deserved.

Elle B. Six

Vegetarian Mentor

Although I had been out of prison for a year, one of the conditions of early release from Camp Reams was that I had to be on probation for two years. I had completed my first year, but I still had one to go. Heading into the probation office was always an eerie feeling because it was the same building where I'd gone to court years ago. Knowing I was in the building where I'd fought for my freedom gave me goosebumps. The halls and elevators had the familiar dark, haunted look even though I was only there to report to the probation department. Heading to the elevator with a long look on my face, I heard a loud, booming voice in the distance. "MR. KING," the voice shouted.

"Stanley Vegetarian! How are you, sir?"

"I'm doing good, but you look like you're doing a whole lot better. How's it feel to be a free man again?"

"It feels great, sir! I'm just here reporting to the probation department. I'm trying to do the right thing, but it's an everyday struggle."

"Well, doing the right thing is hard, son. Doing the wrong thing is easy. Why don't you stop by my office when you're done with probation and we can talk about it?"

"Thank you so much, my brother. I'll see you in a few."

My man Stanley. He saved my life in the courtroom, and he wanted to help me now that I was free. I wasn't sure how he could help me, but I sure would like to catch up with him about my journey. What were the odds of seeing him in a building that was holding about 3,000 people? He was probably the busiest defense attorney in the city, and he was right outside the elevator when I entered the building.

Probation was nothing to me, because I had a job and I was back in college. I was newly married, and I planned to walk the straight and narrow for the rest of my days. I had to report in every month and to take a urine test, but other than that, I lived a normal life. When that was done, I made my way over to see Stanley.

The moment I walked in the door, I could see that Stanley was trying to feel me out to see if I was being honest about turning my life around. "So what you been up to since you been out?"

"Working, going to school, and taking care of the family!"

Surprised by my answer, he questioned me as if I was lying. "Where are you working and where you goin' to school?"

"I'm working at a steel company called Steel Shot and I am enrolled in Cuyahoga Community College. I believe it's your alma mater as well."

"Okay, you did your homework," he said, laughing. "How would you feel about me taking you under my wing?"

"Wow, Stanley, I would love that. I think that would be awesome."

"Listen, Mr. King. It seems you are sincere about turning your life around. I will take you under my wing, but it won't be easy. You can't bullshit me, son. If at any time I believe that you are not giving your maximum effort, I'm going to cut you off. You can decide right now if you want to be the best at what you do, or you can get the hell out of my office."

"I swear I want to be the best, sir, and I will do what it takes. You have my word."

"Well, first thing's first. If you want to prove to me that you're serious, I want grades. I don't want to see you until report card time. You bring me the best grades, and I will help you out, so you've got work to do. If I don't see you again, I will know that you're full of shit!"

It was my mission to prove to Stanley that I was a changed man. I wanted to prove to myself, to my haters, and to the world that I was changed, but I had a huge challenge before me. Going to college was one thing, but getting the best grades when I'd never really taken school seriously was not going to be easy. Getting the best grades, working full time, and being a husband and father meant I would be spread thin, but I could do it.

Bookworm

Grade school was something you had to do because every grownup told you that you must do it to become successful in life, but college was a little different. Not only could you pick your own schedule, but you could pick your own areas of study. College seemed to challenge my mind in a way that my brain gobbled up like food. Elementary school, middle school, and high school were like three quarters of football, and college was the fourth quarter where you could win the game. It was in the fourth quarter where I learned the fundamentals of business, economics, and how to make money. This was where the light bulb went off. If I was going to see the type of money I saw in the drug game, I had to learn what was in those books.

I'd gone through the motions in college before I'd gone to jail, but after I got out, I invested my mind and soul into it. I couldn't believe how much I didn't know. During my first year, I was able to make all A's, and Stanley couldn't be prouder. My hunger for knowledge had even inspired Kelli to go back to college. She was hesitant at first. Her biggest concern was who would fix my meals and take care of me if we were both in school? I assured her I wouldn't starve. School was where we could both make something of ourselves. We had to sacrifice for each other to be great.

My words of encouragement were all she needed to get started. We even made a competition out of it for who could get the highest GPA. After acquiring two degrees from Cuyahoga Community College, it was time for me to move on to university. I gave Kelli grace because she started late, but I held her to the highest of standards. The same pressure Stanley put on me, I put on her. If you wanted to be the best, you had to put in the work.

Stanley was like the father figure I'd always wanted. He was the loudest person at my college graduation. As I walked across the stage, I could look out and see how proud Stanley and my wife were. I would never forget the fact that Stanley had his own life, family, and law practice, but he still took time out of his life to support and mentor me. He had absolutely nothing to gain by doing it, but he took it as seriously as a father with his own son. He didn't let me slack off one bit, and when I was down, he was always there to pick me up. I swear he could only have been sent by God Himself.

DeVry University was a different animal. The curriculum was much more vigorous, but Stanley's demands for excellence had not wavered. The financial structure was a challenge as well. I had to take out some serious student loans to be able to attend. However, I didn't hesitate to take on the financial burden because I knew it would be worth it when I graduated. All I had to do was study hard and make good grades to show that I could do anything in any educational setting.

My first year was complete, and Kelli enrolled in the same school to be by my side. This brought a whole new set of pressures, because I knew I would have to work hard to stay ahead of her in grades. She also had another set of student loans to add to the family's debt. It would be a challenge of epic proportions, but this family was up to the task.

We pushed each other in every way imaginable, and it was beginning to pay off. I completed my bachelor's degree in Technical Management, and Kelli was right behind me with her bachelor's degree in Finance. Although we were drowning in debt, we continued toward our master's degrees. The sky was the limit for the King family, and nothing could stop us now.

The Takeover

By this time, I'd been at Steel Shot for more than five years. I became fascinated by the operation of the different machines. Each of the operators had a specific machine they ran daily. There were employees with tenures of twenty years or more, but none of them had the ability to operate every machine in the facility. Along with the college degrees I acquired, learning all the machines was another way I could set myself apart. I volunteered to learn and run every machine, and while management believed that my motivation was initiative, I had greater aspirations for my actions.

The supervisor in place had given the indication that he planned to retire, and luckily I had all my ducks in a row. I was the only person with a college degree, and I was the only person who could run every machine. It was a long shot since politics always ran deep. There were people who would rather roll over and die before they saw me get that position. There were people who didn't even want the job who were applying for it because they didn't want to take the chance on me getting it.

The supervisor position would be perfect for me. It would give me a chance to earn a better living and give me more flexibility as I was studying for my master's degree. This was going to take a miracle, but I was praying hard for it. If it was in the Lord's will, I would have it. If it wasn't, then I knew the Lord had something better for me.

They called me too young, too black, too loud, and too inexperienced, but now they also called me boss! I got the position. Five years ago, there was only one black machine operator, and five years later, I was the first black supervisor. With greater reward came greater responsibility. Sometimes you had to be careful what you prayed for. Just because you're ambitious doesn't mean that your peers are going to celebrate you. The sharks were circling, so I had to watch my back. I saw that just because people told me congratulations, it didn't mean that they were happy for me.

Graduation Conversation

Kelli and I were more competitive than ever when it came to grades. We pushed each other in every way as we headed toward our graduate degrees. I knew that because I was a convicted felon, I had to produce supreme accolades to stand out in a competitive corporate market. I would have loved to graduate with a 4.0 GPA, but it didn't seem to be in the cards. Kelli's GPA sat at 3.8, while I was lingering at 3.6. I was so proud of her, but I couldn't let it show, because this was still a serious competition. I had to win or I would never live it down. We were going into our final classes and we both had a full schedule with four classes each. We were hitting the books hard, but it was not easy. We had very little time for ourselves and less time for each other. Things were getting tough, but I could take it. The reward of a corporate job felt like it was an arm's length away. I just had to go and get it.

•••

Damn it, she beat me again! Kelli graduated with a 3.82, and I finished with a 3.67. You needed a 3.7 to graduate with distinction. I missed it by .03. Unbelievable! How could this happen? I really needed the distinction on my résumé, but if I hadn't made it, at least my wife had. We were ready to spread our wings and take on this job market. It had been eight years since I'd been released from prison. I held a great job, earned four college degrees, and had a happy marriage. These were the good times. It was time for my life to soar. Soon I would have time to be a better husband, a better father, and a better man.

•••

Kelli and I arrived at the Columbus Auditorium with more excitement than I could ever remember. Kelli had been boasting about having a special surprise for me, but I didn't know what it was. I thought she would give it to me before we left home. When we were in the car I thought she would give it to me. Now that we were at the venue, I was really anxious about my surprise, but the Lord says don't be anxious over anything. The building was black with a shimmering gold roof and was about the size of a football field. We entered through a set of ten-foot Victorian doors and into the grand ballroom. The moment we entered, the beauty of the architecture took my breath away. There was crown molding everywhere. Pictures of angels playing harps were strategically placed throughout. Once we made it to our seats, I froze with confusion. I saw someone sitting there who looked familiar, and by the way she was looking at me, I thought she knew me too. *Is it…no, it can't be?* It was my mom.

Once we locked eyes there was a simultaneous motion. As I walked forward, she was standing to greet me. We captured each other in a tight embrace. We hugged for what felt like an hour as we wept and wept. We tried to compose ourselves because the ceremony was beginning, but I had so many questions. I looked over at Kelli and gave her a playful nudge because she'd got me good on this one. I never could have guessed this.

As they called name after name, I couldn't help but sneak glances at my mom. I feel bad that I didn't recognize her right away, but she had gained a lot of weight since I last saw her. You could tell that she was living her life clean, but she didn't look well health-wise. Although she had gained weight and was clearly battling some health issues, she was as beautiful as I remembered. Her makeup was flawless and her smile could still light up a room. I never would have thought in a million years that I would actually be graduating with my mom proudly watching. This was like a dream come true. It was more than a surprise.

When I stood up to get my degree, I really

felt like I was having my Antwone Fisher moment. Finally, the moment I'd been waiting for:

"David King."

I began walking across the stage and looked out at my wife and mother cheering in the audience. I couldn't compose myself. My eyes  were streaming with tears as I made my way to shake the dean's hand and raise my master's degree. I was so happy I didn't fall because I could not see where I was walking as I made my way down the stairs and back to my seat where they were waiting. As my mom squeezed me with a hug, tears smearing her makeup, I couldn't help feeling that this was an arrangement made by God.

My mom had flown in from Mississippi and took a cab to the ceremony. I was happy to have her ride home with us because I wanted the opportunity to talk to her. They both got in the front seat and I got in the back. The moment we all got in the car, I noticed that Kelli and my mom were still crying. The ceremony was touching but it wasn't that touching.

"What's wrong, y'all? How are you both happier than I am?"

It was a failed attempt at humor because neither of them composed themselves or answered, so I asked again in a concerned tone.

"What's wrong?"

My mom slowly spoke through her tears.

"The reason I am here is because I wanted to see you. I have some serious health issues, and I was afraid that if I didn't come see you now, I would never see you again. There's no easy way to say this so I'm just going to say it. I may have less than three months to live."

I could hardly compose any words as I reached my hand into the front seat and placed it on her shoulder.

"Are you sure, Momma? Have you gotten a second opinion?"

"I'm far beyond a second opinion, son." She lifted her hand and slowly pulled off her wig, revealing a shaved head with a clear tube hanging from her scalp.

Kelli let out a gasp and grabbed my mom's hand. They had formed a bond that I didn't know about. My mom found her on a professional website and let her know she had developed a brain tumor. Although they had never met in person, they stared at each other as if they had known each other for a lifetime. There were too many emotions to deal with in one day. The same day that I received my master's degree, I found out my mom was dying. The same day she came back into my life, I found out she was leaving. This was the happiest and saddest day in my life. I tried to make myself believe that because I didn't have a relationship with my mom, I didn't need her. But I did need her. I didn't want her to die. *This is so unfair.*

• • •

I could not convince my mom to come and live with Kelli and me for her final months. If she was only going to have three months, I would have loved to spend it with her. I had to ask myself, if I was told that I only had three months to live, would I want to spend it in another woman's house? The answer to that question was simple. I wouldn't want to do that. Although I couldn't get her to stay all three months, I talked her into two weeks. It didn't take long for her to return to mother form. She had only been in the house one day and she was already giving me tasks to do. It was nice to have my mom back. She fixed my favorite meal, fried pork chops and corn. When I heard her talk, I realized where I got my sense of humor. When she told a story, she was the funniest lady that I ever heard. After we ate dinner, we went into the living room and sat on the couch. She kicked off the conversation and I finally got up the nerve to ask her how she and my dad met. I was not prepared for her answer.

"First of all, I met yo' old-ass daddy when I was twenty-five and he was thirty-five."

I fell off the couch laughing because I knew what this story was going to be like.

"No wait, listen, son, get up," she said as she also started to laugh. I composed myself and regained my seat on the couch next to her.

"Like I said, your father was ten years older than me. Like any young dumb girl, I believed him when he promised me the world. I was so caught up in his nice cars and money that I didn't care that he was older. I knew that he sold drugs, but it wasn't abnormal for our neighborhood. We were only dating for one month before tragedy struck."

"Tragedy? What tragedy could have happened in one month?"

"Your daddy owned a shoeshine parlor on East 79th and Woodland. There was a cemetery directly across the street. One day I was with your father as he was bringing a garbage bag full of marijuana out of the parlor to put in the trunk of his car. As soon as we got in the car, fifty police officers came running toward us. They were hiding in the cemetery watching his dumb ass."

"Oh my God! What did you do?"

"I was just sitting there looking stupid when out of nowhere your father pulled a small gun out of his pocket."

"WHAT?"

"Yes, child, he pulled out a gun and told me that they were coming for him. Then he told me to hide the gun. I was in such a shock as he set the gun on my lap, that I just grabbed it and put it in my panties."

"Oh no, Ma, you didn't."

"Yes, I did. To make a long story short, they found the gun and took both of us to jail. I was so mad at his ass, but I was madder at myself. All I could think of was how could I be so stupid? I made myself a promise that I was never going to talk to this old-ass crook again."

Chuckling under my breath, I whispered, "I heard that."

"I was so devoted to never talking to him again that I didn't even let him bail me out of jail. I bailed myself out. He tried calling and popping up everywhere that I was, but I wanted nothing to do with him. That's when tragedy struck again."

"Come on, another tragedy already? This has to get better. Y'all had to make me."

"Yeah, we had to make you. You were the next damn tragedy. I missed my period."

We both burst out laughing.

"I'm thinking, ain't no way I'm getting back entangled with this man who just got me thrown in jail." I could tell that she came to a serious part of the story because she paused, stared at me and slowly lowered her head.

"When I found out I was pregnant I threw the pregnancy test in Lake Erie. I was so disgusted with myself that I could hardly eat. I knew that I wasn't going to tell your daddy. I didn't really have a stable home for me to live in, so it would be even more difficult to find a place after I had a baby. That's when I made the fateful decision that I would get an abortion."

"Hold up, hold up, hold up, an abortion? This wouldn't be so shocking if you weren't talking about me here. Momma, you were going to abort me?"

"Yes, son, you asked so I'm gon' give it to you straight. I'm dying so you might as well hear it all. Obviously you were born, so the abortion situation didn't work out. Do you want to hear the story or not?"

We both chuckled through the sharpness of the moment.

"Yes please. I want to hear it all."

The tone turned serious again as she continued.

"I was all scheduled for my abortion, but the morning I woke up to go to the appointment, nothing would go right. First, I couldn't find the keys to my car. Then when I finally found my keys, the damn car wouldn't start. I had to go get the neighbor to help me get the car started. Once the car was started, I was so frustrated that I just sat behind the wheel and yelled at the top of my lungs."

I reached over to hold her hand as her grief overtook her ability to speak.

"Do you want to take a break? I don't want this to become overwhelming."

Through her tears she stumbled on.

"As I screamed in the car, my eyes were so blurry with tears that I could not see out of the windshield. It just looked like a blurry mess. That's when the scariest thing of all happened."

"What?"

"In the middle of the blur I saw an angel. It was a white lady with the deepest blue eyes I had ever seen. She told me that the child that I was carrying would be a boy and that he would be special. My cry turned to awe as she spoke."

"Come on, Ma. Cut the BS. An angel? This story's getting weird."

She completely ignored what I said and carried on.

"As fast as she appeared and told me you were special, she was gone. I wrestled with myself on if I just saw what I thought I saw. I lifted my head to the sky and asked God for guidance. 'If I am supposed to have this baby, please give me a sign because I am lost, Lord.' Although you could not be more than six weeks in my womb, I felt you kick."

She was telling this story with such conviction and emotion that I could not doubt her. I also did not want to interrupt her again.

"From that moment on, my tears dried up and I knew that you would be my angel baby boy. But honey, as you grew up I began to doubt that it was an angel that told me to have you. It was the damn devil!"

We both burst out laughing as she rolled her eyes up in her head for memories.

"Was I that bad?"

"Hell naw, you were worse. Shit! You were a slickster just like yo daddy. I swear that nigga spit you out. You talked shit just like him because you were always around him. You wound up a drug dealer just like him. Mix that with the fact that I had to put up with him sexually harassing me for sixteen years because he was an old pervert. I would say that yeah, that wasn't no damn angel."

Jokingly I said, "Thanks for giving it to me gently."

We shared another tearful laugh as I grabbed us some tissues.

"David, once your daddy was killed and we lost his financial support, I was lost. It was hard enough for me to feed myself, let alone feed, clothe, and house a teenage boy. I lost myself in drugs and didn't care about where you were. Shit, I didn't care where I was. How do you love family when you don't love yourself? Do you understand, baby?"

"I really understand, I do."

We shared a brief hug and she continued.

"I'll tell you one thing, I may have doubted an angel told me to have you until I saw you walking across the stage at that graduation. I looked up at you and said, 'Wow, that's my son.' You lost me and your father when you were just sixteen years old, and I can honestly say that if either one of us were in your life beyond that point, you probably wouldn't have walked across that stage. You are special and I don't know what the Lord's purpose for your life is, but He has protected you. He made you into the man you are today."

"Momma, I gotta tell you that I have a hard time believing that

I'm special. I haven't accomplished anything. What? I went to jail and I went to school. I have a regular job and I'm just one disaster away from bankruptcy."

Cutting me off, she got angry.

"Unh-unh, David, don't you dare put yourself down. Not in front of me. Talking 'bout all you did was go to school. Ain't nobody in my whole damn side of the family graduate from high school. Yo' daddy even quit school in the seventh grade, which means you should be double dumb."

I may not have gotten book smarts from this lady, but my ability to turn a joke definitely came from her. She had my stomach hurting from so much laughing.

"Please, Ma, stop, stop—I can't take it."

"Shit, yo' daddy quit school in the seventh grade, but I don't even think he got all that. I ain't bullshitting. He could count money, but you wasn't never gon' see him reading no newspaper."

"Momma, I'm about to walk outta here because I can't breathe. You have to stop." I rose from the couch and started walking toward the kitchen.

"Okay, okay, okay, I'll stop."

We said we would stop but we both continued with a wordless trade of laughter. Every time I would laugh, it would make her start again and vice versa. What an amazing experience of getting to know my mom before she went on to see the Lord.

What are the odds of me having a graduation at the time of her prognosis? What are the odds that the graduation would bring closure to both of us? What are the odds of her ever being able to tell me the story of my conception? Do I believe her story about an angel telling her to allow me to be born? Not really. But why would she make it up if she's going to die?

See You Later

Taking my mom to the airport was the hardest thing that I ever had to do. This couldn't be the final goodbye. If she wouldn't stay here with me, I would have to go and spend some time with her. Before we made it to the airport, I pulled into a McDonald's and parked.

"Momma, I really want to thank you for coming to see me graduate. I really wish we had a chance to know each other better over the years. I love you more than words can say. I just can't tell you how sorry I am for all..." Overcome with grief, I had difficulty finishing the sentence. My mind went blank with the uncontrollable tears. She sat back and watched in amazement as if she were surprised at my grief. She didn't shed a tear as she looked at me and smiled.

"I want to tell you a story. You know why I named you David King? One of the great heroes of faith is named David. His destiny was great because he went on to become the king of Israel. Even his family didn't believe that there was anything special about him. His destiny was rough because he was a poor lonely shepherd boy. When it came time to face Goliath, he was victorious, but he still had a rough road to the throne. The king at that time was named Saul, and Saul hated that David was revered for defeating Goliath so he spent years trying to kill David. The Lord supernaturally protected David as he spent years hiding in the desert. Saul's disobedience to God ultimately cost him the throne and David became king. I don't know what Goliaths you will face in your life, but no weapon formed against you can prosper. You have to promise me that when your time comes to go for it, you'll seize that moment."

"What in the world are you talking about? I understand the Bible and all that, but what are you talking about?" I looked at her puzzled as I searched for the words.

"When it's time for you to step out of the shadows, promise me you will go for it." She stared at me with a mom-like glare.

"Of course, I promise, but let's finish the conversation in Mississippi because I'm coming down there. I have to get a couple things in order and then I'll be there."

"Are you really coming? You would do that for me?"

"Call me when you land, and we are going to put it together."

"Well, we're not going to say a long goodbye. Let's just say I'll see you later then."

"That sounds like a plan, Ma. I'll see you later."

We embraced and she repeatedly kissed my cheek. I finally knew what it felt like to have a mom. Even though I was thirty years old and I hadn't seen her since I was nineteen, I felt like she had never missed a minute of my life. I pulled her bag from the trunk and handed it to the bellhop at the airport entrance.

"Hey Ma, instead of becoming king, you think the Lord could just bless me with a comfortable, quiet, financially blessed life? Becoming king sounds like too much work."

She burst out laughing as we shared a final hug.

"I'll call you when I land, crazy boy. I love you."

"I love you too."

I rode around for a little while reflecting on the last two weeks. I pulled into the driveway, but I didn't get out of the car. Kelli saw me sitting in the car, so she came out and sat in the car beside me.

"Are you okay?"

"Yeah, I'm good. I was just reflecting on Mom. I didn't even know she went to church, but she is pretty far out there with the Bible."

"Why do you say that?"

"Oh, nothing bad. I'm just saying that before she left she was talking about becoming a king, great destinies, and fighting great fights. Like I said, she is out there a little bit. I guess when you find out you are going to see the Lord, you get extra religious."

"Well, that's one way of looking at it, or she can really believe that you are meant for greatness. I know I think the same thing about you but our belief is not enough. Mr. King, the only way the Lord is going to do great things in your life is if you begin to believe in yourself."

She grabbed the door handle and exited the car without allowing me to say a word.

●●●

I couldn't understand why I could get upset that my mom hadn't called in one day after we'd been out of contact for so many years. She only had a three-hour flight, so she had plenty of time to get settled in. I just wanted to know if she'd made it home safe. *The hell with it, I'm calling.*

Ring, ring.

"Hello?"

"Hey Ma, I just wanted to check in on you, but I see you made it home. Did I catch you at a good time?"

"Who is this? Is this David?"

"Yeah Ma, it's me," I said, chuckling.

"Oh good, this is your cousin Rene and I'm here with your uncle Junior. Come here, Junior, come talk to him."

"Hi Rene, how are you—is everything okay?"

"Uh hey, boy, this is Junior."

"Hello Junior, is everything okay?"

"Uh naw, Dave, your momma sick and didn't none of us know how to get in touch with you."

"What do you mean sick? She just left yesterday. Can I talk to her? Hello…hello?"

"Listen, this is Rene back on the phone. I'm so sorry to tell you this, baby, but when your mother got off the plane, she took a cab home. Once they made it to her house the cab driver couldn't wake her up."

"What? Is she still alive?"

"Yes, she's still alive but she's on life support. Doctors are working tirelessly to figure out what's wrong with her."

My chest began to heave in and out like I was gasping for air and my eyes began to well with tears.

"Oh my God. I'm on my way down there."

Kelli and I booked the next flight to Mississippi. I could not concentrate on anything but Mom being okay. *She only has three months to live and she deserves to have that time. I know she will recover, I just*

Sleeping in the Jungle

know it. There are so many things I need to say to her. There are so many things I want her to say to me. Please, Lord, let her be okay.

•••

When we arrived at the hospital, the sense of relief was overwhelming. Tucked in the first hospital bed of a two-person room was my mom. My cousin Rene was nestled in a chair in the corner with a blanket on top of her. Rene was brown-skinned, petite, and as country as can be. Mississippi style.

"Hello, Rene."

Slowly focusing her eyes, she rose to her feet while fixing her hair to give me a hug.

"Hey baby, you made it. It's so good to see you. You look just like your mother, boy."

"Good to see you too. This is my wife, Kelli."

As the two of them embraced, I walked over to my mom's bedside. Although she was unconscious and hooked to all kinds of machinery, I spoke to her anyway.

"Hey, little lady. Why are you causing all this ruckus? Why don't you wake on up and let's get out of this hospital?"

Just as I finished my statement, a thin-framed Indian man with glasses entered the room.

"Hello, Dr. Phinizee. This is Hannah's son David."

"Fantastic, it is so good to make your acquaintance. We are unable to talk about your mom's medical situation with anyone except her next of kin. Can I step outside and speak with you?"

"Absolutely, you lead the way."

We walked out into the hallway, down the hall to an empty adjacent room.

"I am very sorry to be meeting you this way," Dr. Phinizee said, "but I want to explain to you the severity of the situation that we are facing with your mom. Has she told you about her previous prognosis with her brain tumor?"

It was very hard to understand him because he talked so fast and had a heavy accent, but I caught the important parts of what he had to say.

"Yes, she told me about the brain tumor."

"Oh good, so a lot of what I have to say won't come as a shock to you. We originally informed her that she had three months to live, but that was under her first prognosis. For some reason your mom is having serious complications not related to the brain tumor. She is experiencing heart failure and is showing very little signs of brain activity. The only reason she is alive is because the machines are keeping her alive, but there is simply no possibility she will recover from her current state. You have a very serious decision to make. We can keep her alive for three months, we can keep her alive for a year, or you can make the tough choice to remove her from life support and she can take her final rest. What do you want to do?"

"I am so sorry, but I am not the right person to make that decision. My mom and I only reconnected a couple weeks ago. I will have to talk to the family to get their input. It's not my decision to make."

I slowly began to sit in a chair that was placed in the corner of the empty room and tried to get control of my emotions. *What on earth am I supposed to do? Why does every story in my life have to end tragically? I threw away more than a decade with my mom, and now I will do anything to have five more minutes with her.*

"I understand, Mr. King. Please talk to your family, but unfortunately, the only one who can make the decision is you. You are her next of kin and you have the ultimate authority. I know how difficult this is for you. I will give you some time to think about it."

After speaking with the family, we ultimately made the decision that we would let Mom have her time to rest with the Lord. I agreed, but a part of me did not agree. I just wanted her to come back for one moment so that I could say goodbye. When I dropped her off at the airport, we ended with "see you later" instead of "goodbye" because we thought we had more time. All I wanted to do was say goodbye. The next day we removed the life support and Mom went quietly to the Lord.

Nobody Believes You

I was more than broken up over my mom, but nobody believed me. I was having a difficult time getting over the guilt of things said over the years, things done over the years, lives ignored over the years, yet nobody believed me. Our mother/son relationship had been repaired over a two-week period, but nobody believed me.

I made the arrangements according to her final wishes. She wanted a funeral without a repass. It had always been tradition to have a repass directly after the funeral, and she did not specify her reasoning for not wanting it, but I respected her wishes. As arrangements went out, everyone was confused. *Why isn't there a repass?* I explained my mom's wishes over and over, but nobody believed me.

I never got a chance to say goodbye to my mom, so it was my intention to get up at the funeral and say my final goodbye. I walked out on the elevated platform and poured my heart out. I cried, reminisced, and apologized through my tears, but nobody believed me. To them my tears were as fake as a three-dollar bill. In their eyes we hadn't liked each other our whole lives. If I were to tell them that she thought I was an angel, they would never believe me. If I told them that she thought I was someone destined for greatness, they would never believe me.

There was only one audience member that I needed to believe me and that was my mom. She was there in spirit and hung on every word I spoke. It was never meant for us to say goodbye; we were only meant to say see you later. We will see each other later. Later in heaven. I promised my dad that if I was ever in trouble I would call out to the Lord. I also promised him that I would get an education. I kept those promises. I began to reflect on the promise that I made my mother. She made me promise that if I ever saw an opportunity to go for it, I would. *I must keep that promise and I will.*

OBAMA EFFECT

When you had your head buried in work, college, and life, you had very little time to pay attention to the world going on around you. The loss of my mother had also put me in a daze for the next year. There was a presidential election going on, and the candidate was a black man. I didn't ever remember race relations being that bad. The polarization of the times had people losing their minds. Friends who were close to you were no longer your friends because of politics. It was also the worst time in the world to be looking for a job. I had applied to every company in northeast Ohio, and nothing. I couldn't even get past a first interview. I had a pretty good job at Steel Shot, but I knew I needed more once my student loans went into repayment. They called it the "great recession," but I called it buzzard luck. How could the entire economy tank after I graduated from college? I was in trouble.

One of the great blessings was that the great recession hadn't disrupted Kelli's pursuit of a good job. She was able to land a six-figure job within six months of graduating college with her master's degree. Our financial burdens had been eased for the time being, but I was getting discouraged about my job prospects. Interview after interview, companies were in love with my work history and college degrees, but they couldn't get past my criminal record.

Buffet of Advice

Come on, God! I know You didn't bring me this far to have me falter. No matter how hard I tried, I couldn't find a higher-paying job. My student loans were killing me, and I was becoming a burden on Kelli's income. Of course, she was not saying anything because we were married and all that we had belonged to the both of us, but I felt terrible. The economy was losing 200,0000 jobs per month, so I knew it wasn't just me who couldn't find a job, it was everybody. I had to find a way. I had to ask God for help. *Please, God, show me a way!*

I did research on how to prosper in a financial crisis and ran across an interview with billionaire Warren Buffet. There was a long way between a billionaire and what I had, but it wouldn't hurt to listen.

The reporter asked Mr. Buffet, "What can people do to get ahead in these hurtful economic times?"

He replied, "People should buy houses, fix them up, and rent them out."

When I read the comments, I saw that there was very little respect for what Mr. Buffet had to say. People were trashing him. One comment said how out of touch he was to give advice to buy houses when so many people were losing their jobs and didn't know where their next meal was coming from. Attack after attack, and not one positive comment. Of course, that kind of advice was not for everyone, but it was the kind of advice that could be beneficial for middle class people with means. I had about $150,000 in my 401K, and I could borrow up to 50 percent of that without penalty. *Why would Mr. Buffet give that advice unless he thought it would help?* Intrigued, I had no choice but to continue researching this new-found advice.

Real estate foreclosures were skyrocketing in inner-city Cleveland; houses were selling dirt cheap. Unfortunately, when people lost their homes, they didn't just walk away and hand over the keys. They tore out all the plumbing, fixtures, electrical, pretty much anything they could sell. After they were done, the crackheads came in and stole the rest. It was going to be risky trying to start a business in that environment. All I could afford were houses in bad neighborhoods. In those neighborhoods, life was very inexpensive. You could easily get hurt in the hood before the financial crisis, but after the crisis hit, even the kids were dangerous.

I got a check for $75,000 out of my retirement savings. I felt like a real estate tycoon already. You know how people act when they got a few dollars? You couldn't tell me anything! I bought my first house for $6,500. It was a real dump and needed a total remodel, but it had potential. The first thing I looked for in rental property was size, because people loved space. If you had a lot of space, you would never have trouble finding a tenant. My new property had two houses on the same lot. A two-family up front with five bedrooms upstairs and three bedrooms down. It was massive. There was also a single-family house in the rear. Not bad for $6,500.

Blind Letter

I couldn't put all my eggs in one basket. Until I started making money from real estate, I still needed to look for a better-paying job. At this point, my hard work and higher education felt like it was for nothing. My criminal record was keeping me from getting the job my education should demand. Master's degree, managerial experience, on the same job for twelve years, and I couldn't get past the first interview. How could I afford my student loans on the wage I made at Steel Shot? This was ridiculous. They told you when you got out of jail if you turned your life around, you could still be successful, but that was because they didn't expect you to do it. The pieces of paper my degrees were printed on were not good for anything except toilet paper. *God, why would You let me waste all that time and money chasing a corporate job, when nobody wants me?* They couldn't care less that I had graduated at the top of my class and that I hadn't had so much as a parking ticket since I'd gotten out of jail. All they saw was a felon.

My frustration hit a new high. It was taking me an eternity to rehab the house I'd bought because I had zero experience. My inexperience was what led me to underestimate how much work needed to be done to get the house habitable. The only thing I had was the ability to write. I sent out over a hundred letters asking for advice, help, guidance, anything that could help me get past my dilemma. I emailed every black organization, the councilmen, the top fifty richest people in the world, top athletes, and even the President. *Isn't anyone out there willing to listen to a man who just wants to be somebody? Is anyone out there? I need help or I'm finished.* I needed a miracle.

One hundred messages sent around the world, and ninety-nine of them didn't respond. There was only one person who received my letter, read it, and bothered to respond. Her name was Denise, and she was the president of a black organization called Stand Up here in Ohio. She was intrigued by the passion inside my letter and stated that she wanted to help. I could meet her at her downtown office on Monday.

Denise Strong

Denise was a heavy-set brown-skinned woman who got around on an electric scooter. She could walk just fine, but she had diabetes, and the scooter helped her when she had problems with her legs. She was not disabled by any means, and she commanded any room she entered. Denise was the executive director of all African-American business organizations in the county. She was the kind of lady who never accepted "no" for an answer and could make her way through a crowd of a million. When President Obama came to town, she drove her scooter through the massive crowd as if she was on a mission. She set out to get a hug from the President and to take a picture with him, and she could not be denied. When I watched her network and work a room, she moved as gracefully as a butterfly. Her famous quote from the Bible was, "You have not because you ask not." If you wanted it, you had to pray for it, then go out and get it.

Sleeping in the Jungle

Denise kept me by her side everywhere she went. I took notes for her as she negotiated sponsorships from the largest organizations in the country. When we were at executive events, she pointed people out and told me to go over and shake their hands. "Introduce yourself with a firm handshake and hold your shoulders back. Always look a man in his eyes when you speak, and listen more than you talk." I used to get nervous at events, thinking I didn't belong. Denise taught me to enter a room like the most important person in the room, and my confidence would resonate.

One day over lunch, I saw that Denise was feeling extra motherly. She hugged me tight out of nowhere and said, "Do you know that everything is going to be all right?"

"Of course," I responded, but my voice cracked with doubt.

"Have you ever thought about getting your criminal record expunged?"

"Actually, I have thought about it, but unfortunately I can't because I have more than one felony."

"Really? That's unfortunate. Are you sure there's no way to get it expunged?" she asked as if she already knew the answer.

"Yes, there is. The governor could issue me a pardon or executive clemency. Out of a governor's four-year term, they usually issue about ten out of a hundred thousand petitions for pardon, so in other words, it is impossible to achieve."

"Why impossible? You just said he hands out ten out of a hundred thousand. It is only impossible if you believe that it's impossible. Nothing is impossible for the God I serve. If you pray for it and He doesn't bless you with it, you don't need it. Why don't you find out what you need to do to petition the governor? The worst thing he could say is no."

She was right. I shouldn't have been so quick to discount the possibility of a governor pardon. However, I'd researched pardons previously, and I knew they didn't give out pardons for drug convictions. In the past, those were only given to people in the form of commuted sentences after someone had been in jail for many years.

I figured out the process, but it was more than a long shot, and I think she knew it. We prayed for it together, and I remained optimistic.

Sold To The Brother In Need

The annual Stand Up executive auction was where top executives in Cleveland would allow their time to be auctioned to the highest bidder. Some executives offered eighteen holes of golf, others offered a mentorship lunch, and some offered the opportunity to meet them at their office. If it wasn't for the executive auction, it would be extremely difficult to spend time with the individuals participating in this event. Not only was I responsible for the auction logistics, but I also set up the meetings between the winning bidders and executives. Denise had already identified the person I needed to bid on. He was an executive at a top construction firm and was responsible for building skyscrapers all over the world. His name was Turner Smith, and he was not going to go cheap in the auction. I didn't care what it cost; I was going to win.

The auction was an absolute success. Not only did we raise a lot of money for charity, but I won my bid for Turner Smith. I didn't know what I was going to say when I met him. Not only was he the senior VP of Atlantic Construction, but he was also a civil rights icon and ordained minister. Although we had very little in common, I couldn't let that sway me from my corporate ambitions. I knew that he held the keys to opening my future, and it was imperative that I got him to see it also.

Sleeping in the Jungle

As I arrived at the tall office building in downtown Cleveland, I prayed for the right words to say. I stepped out of the elevator on the thirty-third floor and was floored by the high-end décor. There was granite as far as the eye could see. After the secretary made a quick call, Turner Smith appeared from the back side of a glass corridor. Standing 6'5" inches tall, he looked like an NBA player walking toward me. I couldn't believe it—we had on identical black suits and blue ties.

"Hello, Mr. King. How are you, sir?"

"I am doing fantastic, Mr. Smith. It is an honor to meet you."

"Mr. King, it looks like you got my email on what to wear." He hit me with a huge grin.

"Either that, or you were peeping in my windows last night," I quickly replied.

Out of nowhere came the loudest laugh that echoed off every wall in the lobby.

Not wanting to miss an opportunity when I had the brother laughing, I hit him with one more. "Don't really matter what time you came to the house. You would have seen it, because I tried the suit on eighty-six times before I went to sleep."

Mr. Smith was beside himself laughing. It might not have been appropriate to be so loose when initially meeting an executive, but he cracked a joke with me first. "Come on in my office, Mr. King. Let's get to know each other."

This guy's office was out of this world—a panoramic view of the entire city with one set of windows filled with Lake Erie in the distance. I had no idea what to make of Turner Smith. He was the nicest man I had ever met in my life. Not only did he give me encouragement, but the longer I sat in our meeting, the more I believed I could do anything I put my mind to. After I reluctantly shared my frustrations about my past, he took none of that into account. He referred to my frustrations as excuses.

"The only things that will be a roadblock in your future are things you allow to be a roadblock. To overcome adversity, you must have superior attitude, superior work ethic, and a superior presence." He loved my ambition. He had inspired me to consider that I had more positive things to offer than I gave myself credit for. I had four college degrees, a great family, and a good job. Some people worked their whole lives to accomplish those things, and I had done them all after being out of prison for twelve years.

"Do you have a tuxedo?"

"No, sir, I don't," I responded, confused.

"Well, you need to rent one then. Let me know if you don't have the money to do so and I will make arrangements for you."

"I can afford to rent one, but what do I need it for? Are we going to a wedding?"

Humored by my innocence, he laughed hysterically. "You wouldn't need a tuxedo for a wedding unless you were in the wedding. I want you to be my guest for a black-tie dinner I am giving for some business leaders in the city. It will give you an opportunity to mingle among the elite and demonstrate some of the superior traits I'm going to teach you. Are you ready for the big time?"

"Yes, sir, I am."

"Are you sure?"

"I am very sure."

"Well, let's go make it happen, Brother King."

Black-Tie Affair

Despite all the things Denise had going on, she was instrumental in helping me complete my application for a pardon by the governor. Stanley Vegetarian also proofread my petition and added some verbiage of his own. The greatest part of the situation was that Turner Smith wrote me a personal letter of recommendation.

Everyone was optimistic over the quality of our petition, but I decided to add a personal message. My application illustrated my accomplishments, my goals, and my connections, but it lacked the true insight into who I was. In order to represent that, I had to show where I'd come from. That was when I wrote a story about a little boy sleeping in the jungle gym. I told what happened to my dad, my mom, and the circumstances that led me to criminal behavior. It was uncertain how anyone who read the letter would interpret it, but I felt it was necessary to be completely transparent.

The black-tie dinner was something I'd only seen on TV. There were celebrities, business leaders, and a complete who's who in the city. One thing was for certain—I felt like a social misfit. I was sitting at a table by myself and absorbing everything going on around me. Watching Turner work the room was like a movie. It was inspiring to see a black man have so many people jockeying for his time. He was not a celebrity from an entertainment standpoint, but he had the "it" factor. Whatever "it" was, he definitely had it.

Damn, he spotted me sitting by myself. Now here he comes.

"Brother King, come with me. I have some people I want you to meet."

My heart sank as I rose from the table. All I could tell myself was to smile and follow Turner's lead. He walked around the room introducing me to people, forcing me to interact, and it wasn't long until I was right at home. Nobody in here knew who I was, what was in my past, or the fact that I felt I didn't belong. What they saw was a well-groomed black man in a tuxedo who was with one of the top business people in the city. All I had to do was be myself.

"Brother King, I have one final person I want you to meet."

"No problem. Let's go."

We made our way across the room and approached a couple of well-groomed men with earpieces in their ears. Turner answered a couple of quick questions from the gentlemen, and just like that I was standing face to face with someone I couldn't believe was in front of me.

"Brother King, I would like to introduce you to Governor Tom Freedom."

Oh my God, it can't be! The governor of Ohio. The man who held my fate in his hand. *What should I say? What should I do?* I knew I should definitely say something, but all I could do was stare. *Get yourself together.* He was just a man like anybody else. He was reaching out his hand to shake mine, so I had to do something.

"Hello, Governor. I can't tell you what a pleasure it is to meet you."

"Likewise, young man. Turner here hasn't been giving you any trouble, has he?" As the two men laughed, I wasn't sure if I should also.

"No, sir, he hasn't given me any trouble, but he knows how much I admire you and he wanted me to meet you. Would you mind if I take a picture with you?"

"If you admire me that much, then I will definitely take a picture with you."

As Turner stood back to take the photo, I couldn't help thinking that I must be the most blessed guy in the world. Only God could arrange a meeting with me and the governor after I prayed so hard that he would pardon me. The governor was very busy, so after the picture he was quickly whisked off to meet other people.

"Wow, Brother Turner. How can I ever repay you for tonight?"

"Repay me for what? I haven't done anything yet. There are a lot of people who need me to do things for them, but I feel moved to help you, and that's what I'm going to do."

"Thank you, sir. Thank you very much."

I woke up the next day and couldn't stop thinking about my perfect evening. You would've thought that meeting the governor would be the thing that stuck out in my head the most, but it wasn't. What stuck out was Turner saying that he felt moved to help me. *Why would he say that?* Turner and I had closed out the night with a prayer that asked that the Lord's will be done with my life and that I receive everything I needed to fulfill my destiny. If only I knew what my destiny was.

BOARD OF EVERYTHING

Turner and I became the best of friends. Some would see us as an odd couple of friends because he was in his late sixties and I was in my early thirties, but we had a blast together. We went to sports games together and we always stopped to have dinner at one of his membership clubs before the game. He was another father figure to me, just like Stanley. I always used to see men at the games with their fathers and had wondered what it would be like to have that experience. With Turner, I got to live that experience. He didn't realize how much his mentorship helped me develop. He coached me, Stanley coached me, Denise coached me, and they all did it because they saw the potential in me—a potential I didn't even see in myself, but I was learning.

The first step in getting a pardon by the governor was your petition going through the Ohio Parole Board. After nearly a year and a half of waiting, I finally got a response from them. I was so afraid to open the letter because I had everything riding on it. It was the answer I needed to find out if I had a chance at redemption. It would determine if I ever had a future in corporate America. I could hardly contain myself.

I had to say a quick prayer before I opened it. I knew God was with me, so I had to go through the proper channels. "Lord, thank You so much for the good news that's in this letter. Thank You for a good recommendation and bringing me one step closer to my goal of executive clemency. In Your son Jesus Christ's name, Amen."

Concluding my prayer, I ripped open the letter, and after making it through a lot of legal jargon, I got down to the gist of the letter: "It is the recommendation of the Ohio Parole Board that your petition for executive clemency be hereby denied by Governor Tom Freedom. Although our decision is not binding and the governor has sole pardon power, it is our recommendation that your petition be blocked. In the event that you are denied by the governor, you cannot resubmit your petition for two years after your date of denial."

Just like that, my whole world was crushed. I couldn't believe I'd done all that work for nothing. All that praying, all those dinners, searching people out, all that networking, all for nothing. I was right back in the same situation I'd been in when I'd started my journey. A black man with four college degrees who couldn't get a job to afford his student loans. What a crock.

Shaken Faith

I was so embarrassed to tell my mentors and all the people who believed in me that our efforts had failed. Although the governor pardoned about ten people every four years, he hadn't pardoned anyone who did not gain the recommendation of the parole board. I only wanted to acquire gainful employment and become a productive member of society. How could I achieve that when my past was holding me hostage?

Brother Turner would know what to do. I wanted to get his insight, and the moment I arrived at his office, he could tell something was wrong.

"Well, they turned me down, my brother. It's all over."

"What's over, son?"

"The pardon. We got turned down by the parole board, and the governor takes their recommendation one hundred percent of the time, so we're done."

"You know what, Brother King? Maybe we are done. I can tell you for a fact that if you didn't get this pardon, then the Lord didn't give it to you for a reason. If He didn't give it to you then you don't need it to fulfill your destiny. Is this how you plan to approach things when they don't go your way?"

Although it was the opposite of what I was expecting to hear, I knew Turner was right. I had God with me, and if He didn't give it to me, I didn't need it. "You know what, Turner? You're right. I just have to find another way."

I could see the disappointment and frustration in Turner's eyes. He was not disappointed with the letter, but with me. "Oh, ye with little faith. I'm not sure about the God you serve, but the God I serve is not bound by numbers. You mean to tell me that the God who flung the stars and the moon into the sky, the God who built the world in seven days, the one who's in charge of it all cannot move beyond the hundred-percent failure rate of the parole board? God is in control of the parole board, the governor, you, me, and the President for that matter. You have a lot to learn about faith, young man."

The Promotion

If there was one silver lining to my professional career, it was Steel Shot. They loved the ground I walked on. I'd made my way up the ranks in the company over the past twelve years, and I finally had an opportunity to move into a front office position. If I couldn't climb the corporate structure in another company, I had to just continue to climb where I was.

Our production manager was retiring after a long career on the job, and I was his natural replacement. He always used to tell me that I was the future of the company. After several trips down to the corporate office for interviews, it seemed I was on my way to the front office. No more listening to machines run all the time. No more smelling like oil. I was looking forward to more responsibility and better pay.

I did it! I got the job. I couldn't believe it. I couldn't wait to take my promotion letter home to show Kelli. She was going to be so proud of me. I could see the happiness on her face as she read the letter. I'd done all that complaining about my failures and had never taken the time to realize how blessed my situation was.

While she was reading the letter, I saw her face slowly turn from happiness to worry. "Did you read this letter in its entirety?"

"No, I just saw that it says congratulations, you got the job."

"I saw that too, but it also says at the bottom that this promotion is granted but will be contingent on the results of a successful background check."

My heart skipped a beat. "Background check? Why would they do a background check if I already work for them?"

Kelli's face turned to a look of terror. "It's a part of the corporate structure. When you take a corporate job, you have to have an official background check. Didn't you leave out your criminal past when you got hired?"

"Hell yeah I left it out, or I never would have gotten hired." What was I going to do? I decided to tell them that I wanted to pull out of the promotion for personal reasons.

I walked into work the next day and made a beeline to the plant manager's office, but I didn't make it that far. As soon as I walked into the building, I was called to Conference Room A. My mind began to race. I could hardly breathe as I tried to think of a plausible explanation in case they'd run my background check already. I sure hoped they hadn't organized a congratulatory party for me, because I had to pull out of the promotion.

As soon as I stepped into the conference room, I could already see the writing on the wall. Once I saw the VP of human resources, I knew it was over. He was a 5'2", slightly balding white man we'd nicknamed the bald-headed reaper. If you saw him sitting in a room you were walking into, you were getting fired for sure.

True to form, they let me go. Thirteen years ago, I'd committed a crime that sent me to prison for eleven months, but it may as well have been a life sentence. How could things get this bad so fast? I was previously concerned about how difficult it was for me to climb higher, but now I seemed to be moving backward. No pardon, and then no job. I knew better than to tempt the devil by asking what else could happen. *Lord, I know You have something great in my future, but at this point I need to ask You to bring it to light, because everything I have going for me looks really bad. Here we go again. I need help.*

Lean On Buffet

I had to have the worst luck in the world to have a promotion be the reason I lost my job. After twelve years, why couldn't Steel Shot see past my record and recognize that I was honest and always performed well? They liked me so much that they'd promoted me several times, but because I used to sell drugs when I was twenty, they no longer had a use for my services. *Where were You on that one, Lord?* My faith had been growing day by day, and things had turned into one disappointment after another. First the pardon, then unemployment. I didn't know what I was going to do.

Listening to the advice of Warren Buffet had led me to purchase three properties. Since I had no job and a lot of time on my hands, I had to use Mr. Buffet's advice full time. The only good thing about losing my job was that now I could pull my entire 401K retirement savings. It was nice to have a lump sum of cash on hand, but I knew that it wasn't Monopoly money. It was retirement money, so I had to use it for my future.

I was in the market to buy properties that were in my price range, so I had to continue to invest in the toughest neighborhoods in the city. Drugs and violence were around every corner in these neighborhoods, and life was cheap. In order to be successful there, I had to keep my nose down, get in fast, and get out faster. I had a master plan and $150,000. It was time to see if Mr. Buffet could lead me to prosperity.

Buying properties in rough neighborhoods was tricky because just as you begin moving new materials in the front door, crackheads would be moving your materials out the back door. The trick was to establish electrical service first. Once I had lights, I propped up an old TV set by the window and let it stay on overnight to look like someone was living in the house. Next, I established heat and hot water. That was where you needed to be crafty, because furnaces and hot water tanks were expensive. Once I installed them, I paid someone to physically stay in the house until we finished the renovations.

Because I'd learned that most tenants were looking for larger-sized units, I only bought large multi-unit properties with three bedrooms or more. Once I got one of the units fully rehabbed, I found a tenant to move in. I worked on the connected unit while the other was occupied. It was a pretty good system and had led to me buying ten more properties.

Each property that I bought represented more positive cash flow after expenses. After just one year of real estate investing, I made three times the money that I'd made at Steel Shot. How in the world was that possible? When you really put the story together carefully, it seemed the Lord knew exactly what He was doing by allowing me to get fired in the first place. With the help of God and advice from Warren Buffet, I was on my way to financial independence. I set a goal to buy fifty properties over the next five years and live the rest of my life as a rent collector. Considering I only owned ten properties, I was going to have to put in some serious work to get another forty under my belt.

The Landlord's Here

I was in my fourth year and reaching my thirtieth property. I was clearly going to fall short of my goal of fifty, but I was comfortable with that. I saw that being a landlord was not what it was cracked up to be. The landlord was the most hated man in America. You were the person who came around every month and took all of Mommy's money away. You represented why kids couldn't get a PlayStation for Christmas. You represented why Mommy had to work so much. If Mommy didn't have enough money for rent, you were the man who was going to put them out on the streets. With thirty multi-family properties, there were at least sixty families who hated my guts.

You would not believe the extremes people would go through to avoid paying rent. "It took too long for you to come fix my sink, so I don't have the rent." "My grandfather passed away, so I don't have the rent." "My son got shot, so I don't have the rent." "I don't have the rent this month. Are there some sexual favors I could give you instead?"

One fantastic reason for not paying rent after another. I had an ambition to get to fifty properties, but I now was not sure I wanted that many. Constantly arguing with people over rent and performing maintenance on each property was a monthly challenge. Some people used to say that I needed to find better tenants, but better tenants didn't want to live in those neighborhoods. I had to suck it up and continue on, but it was a daily struggle.

At full occupancy, I brought in more money than I'd ever anticipated, but I was hardly ever at full occupancy. I lived in eviction court. It took two months to evict someone from your property, and then they tore your place up when they left. They pissed on your carpet, wrote on your walls, and sabotaged the plumbing. One lady I evicted was the most ignorant person I'd ever dealt with in my life. I constantly had to explain to her why she couldn't have ten people sleeping over at her house every week. I was responsible for the water bill, and if she had ten people sleeping over, that represented ten extra showers, thirty more toilet flushes, thirty more hand washings, and so on. Her argument was that she could do whatever she wanted in her house if she paid rent. Trying to reason with an ignorant person was like experiencing childbirth through the hole of a penis. It was painful!

I wanted to dance a jig once I had her out of my property, but before I could celebrate, I needed to figure out why water was backing up in the basement of the house. I attempted to snake the drain out, but it didn't seem to be working. I knew she wouldn't go quietly without breaking something, but I didn't know what the hell she'd done to the plumbing. I had a plumber come out, and I had to give it to that girl for originality. *She got me good on this one.* The plumber told me she'd thrown powdered cement down the cleanout drain in the basement. Every time water mixed with it, it just got harder and harder. I had to

Sleeping in the Jungle

pay someone to come and dig up the basement floor and replace all the pipes under the foundation of the house. *I swear the Lord is doing a work in me, but if I see this lady in the streets, it's going to be a beat down! I don't care if I'm dead and gone. If I see her in the line before the pearly gates to get into heaven, I'm kicking her ass! That commotion in line is going to be me trying to rip every hair out of her scalp.*

Another thing I'd never anticipated was the fact that a twenty-thousand-dollar house was not going to have the most stable foundation. Owning thirty of these deteriorating monstrosities was draining the profits in a major way. I was constantly fixing leaky roofs, leaky basements, drafty windows, doing electrical upgrades and plumbing upgrades, replacing furnaces, hot water tanks, and countless other things. I wish I would have grown my business slower by buying higher-quality houses that attracted better tenants. Learning that reality that late in the game could very well equal my demise. I needed to start working on a backup plan.

Laugh to Keep from Crying

I was seventeen when baby Laura was born, and now she was seventeen. Where in the world had the years gone? Since she'd come into this world, I had been homeless, imprisoned, a factory supervisor, a four-time college graduate, and real estate investor. I had spent the greater part of her life chasing redemption and success. Although I had put my efforts into a lot of places, the one thing I hadn't been was a father.

I spent so much time chasing dreams that I'd totally missed her childhood. I provided for her financially and spent several weekends with her throughout each year, but money did not take the place of a father. I could get down on myself, but I had not totally neglected my duties. When she was at school, I was too. When she got out of school, I was on my way to work. Her mom didn't want me to take her every weekend, so I was limited to every other weekend. Life did not allow me to be in two places at one time, but the distance between Laura and me was the size of the Grand Canyon.

By the time I became a successful real estate investor and had more time to spend with her, she had grown accustomed to being without me

Sleeping in the Jungle

in her life. I begged her to give me another chance and start over, but she was hardened to the core. She was seventeen, and her visits every other weekend had dwindled to no weekends. I tried to stress the importance of hard work, education, and faith, but anything I put forward was instantly met with rejection. Her common quote toward me was, "Where were you in my life?"

I didn't know how to answer that question, because I thought I had always been there.

One thing I had to learn was that when someone doesn't want anything to do with you, you can't make them. She still wanted me to help pay for her prom and graduation costs, but she did not want me to attend. I had never been a present father in her life, so I reluctantly accepted my role as the financial dad. I would rather be the financial dad than nothing at all. I might not have made the best parental decisions in my life, but I did the best I could the only way I knew how. I just wished she loved me the way I loved her. It's funny how when you are coming to the end of a story, you think about the beginning. I still remembered the first day she came home from the hospital. So small and innocent, reaching up and depending on me for everything she needed. I could remember the smell of milk on her breath as she slept on my chest. When I closed my eyes, I could hear the rhythm of her heartbeat. Every time I looked in the mirror, I saw her because our faces were so much alike. My prayers had always included one day being able to give her the world. Maybe the Lord didn't want me to give her the world. Maybe this was God's way of telling me she could earn her way to conquering the world on her own so she would appreciate it more. I had to let her live and learn.

Elle B. Six

Stand Up For Yourself

Now that my interest in building a larger real estate empire had dwindled, I had to find a new way to earn a living. I told Kelli I would like to try my hand at show business. I always wanted to be an actor and I always loved stand-up comedy, so I thought I would explore both and see what stuck.

I was a small-time real estate investor nobody had ever heard of, but I wanted to make a name for myself. Ever since I was a small child I had always been able to make people laugh. Maybe that was it. I needed to try stand-up comedy, and that could give me a platform to become successful in show business. The only question was, how do I do that? I only made people laugh in conversations and at parties. I didn't even know if I would be good at comedy, but I had to try. There were plenty of small comedy clubs I had visited in the past. Some of them even had open mic nights, and although they were usually low quality, it was where a wanna-be comedian could find out if he had potential. What did I have to lose? If I was going to be a famous comedian, I had to begin somewhere.

For me to get on stage, I couldn't get drunk, but I had to have something. There was no way I could get up there sober. I absolutely detested illegal drugs, but I thought I might try something that was legal. I'd heard about people smoking synthetic marijuana. It didn't have any THC that could get you high, but people said you got a good head rush. The local head shops everywhere sold it and it was relatively inexpensive. I had low expectations of the effects, but at least I would have something before going on stage. I thought I had written a decent routine and I was ready to make my debut. Open mic night only gave you five minutes, so you had to make the most of it.

On my first open mic night, I smoked nearly all the fake weed I'd

bought. I didn't know if I was high or not, but I knew that my nerves were out of control. It felt like a million ants were dancing inside my stomach. The comedy club only had about fifty people scattered throughout a place that should have held two hundred. The lights were dim everywhere except for the bar and the stage. The stage had a single microphone stand and a wooden stool. It was nothing but the comedian and the audience. I was the third comedian going up that night, and the first two were awful. Barely a chuckle through each of their routines. I felt like I wanted to run out of the place, but I couldn't. I had to try. *The hell with it. I'm going for it!*

I chose the name Chinaman because my wife had given it to me. It was also a hell of a name for a black man. Besides, who wanted to hear jokes from a brother named David? I sure wouldn't. *Oh boy, here comes the MC to call me up.*

"OUR NEXT COMEDIAN COMING TO THE STAGE—PUT YOUR HANDS TOGETHER FOR CHINAMAN." As the audience clapped for a comedian named Chinaman, suddenly a black man walked up on the stage, and the clapping slowed with confusion.

That was when I made it to the microphone and yelled, "SURPRISE."

In that moment, the most amazing thing happened. The crowd erupted with laughter. I was standing on the stage with all eyes focused on me and everyone hanging on my every word. The laughter was like a cool breeze on a hot summer day. Each laugh was like having an orgasm over and over again. The louder the laugh, the more intense the orgasm. I had never felt anything like that. There wasn't any drug, any experience, or any accomplishment that had ever compared to it. I was an absolute smash, and the crowd loved me. In that moment, in that comedy club, I fell in love with laughter. I wanted to be a star.

SYNTHETIC MIND

Everywhere I went, I found myself thinking of different things I could use as jokes. I borrowed material from past comedians. I borrowed material from current comedians. Anything I saw that could get laughs on stage, I used it. I was attacking stages all over the city and beyond, but it wasn't easy. There were a million comedians lobbying for stage time, and they didn't take kindly to newcomers.

Sleeping in the Jungle

The one thing that set me at ease wherever I went was my synthetic weed. I doubted its potency when I'd first begun to use it, but now I swore by it. I smoked it all day, and it put me into a carefree state. I loved how it made me feel. I even smoked it in public, and no one even knew what I was smoking. It gave me amazing stamina because I wrote and performed comedy on the weekends and never got tired. It made me feel invincible.

It seemed like the more I smoked, the more arrogant and brash I became. I had found my voice on stage as the celebrity-hating comedian because I always cracked jokes about the rich and famous. I had begun to build a name on it. I traveled from city to city telling jokes about any and every celebrity. Some of my attacks on celebrities had even become malicious. The foggier my mind became, the further I went with my attacks.

The fake weed had me totally separated from reality. Everyone around me, including my wife, told me that when I smoked it, I turned into a different person. I brushed off any criticism, thinking that anything you could buy at the corner store couldn't be as bad as everyone was making it out to be. I smoked it because I liked it and it helped me feel comfortable when I was on stage. No one was going to be complaining when I became famous. They needed to just let me do me.

Funny as Hell

My platform was beginning to grow, and I had only been doing comedy for two years. I was able to get on some big-time shows because of one of the funniest guys I had ever met. His name was "Funny as Hell." Funny as Hell had been around the comedy scene for many years and had performed on stage with several established comedians dating back decades. He was a dark-skinned black man who stood about 5'9" and had a thick Southern accent. He was a high-energy comedian who made it difficult for any performer to follow him. That was why I believed he was falling on hard times. He was so high energy and so funny that he sucked the energy out of the crowds, and no one wanted to work with him. With me, all that was about to change.

Funny as Hell had the connections so he could get the gigs, but I was a nobody with no connections looking for a shortcut to the top. I made him an offer he couldn't refuse. If he was able to get paid gigs for us anywhere in the country, I would pay for our travel to get there, and out of whatever I got paid as his featuring act, he could have my share. He got the money, and I got stages.

He was getting us so many shows that I was able to work continuously on my craft. I was really starting to get good. I killed it every time I did jokes about famous celebrities. I began to get noticed by comedy clubs around the country and it felt amazing, but through my haze of synthetic weed and constant celebrity attacks, I didn't see a storm brewing ahead. A storm that had the ability to bring the house down.

Uh-Oh

Broadway! Broadway! I was performing in NYC on Broadway. I hadn't been to New York since my drug-dealing days, and now I was there performing on Broadway. I'd never imagined my light could shine so fast, but it was really happening. However, as they said in boxing, "The punch that knocks you out is the one you don't see." Throughout my time of making fun of powerful celebrities and vocalizing those jokes on video, I didn't see that there were some people who felt disrespected. Before I knew it, I had enemies. Rather large enemies who felt like the disrespect needed to stop. Through my synthetic haze, I didn't heed those warnings. In fact, I did the complete opposite. I doubled down on the disrespect because I believed I had finally made a name for myself—something I had been trying to do for years. Every time someone took a shot at me, I took a bigger shot at them from the stage. It felt like a game, but for some reason I was the only one having fun.

They say the more attention you get, the more problems come your way, and I now knew what that meant more than ever. My comedy career came under fire for some of my actions on stage. It seemed that when you used the material of other comedians, it was like committing an act of treason in the comedy world. I couldn't say that I didn't know that. I had been warned many times about it, but when I was just getting started, I always rationalized that I was doing what I had to do to get stage time. I never knew my star would rise that fast, and comedians around the country began yelling

bloody murder. I had written a great deal of my own routine, but the things I'd borrowed were truly problematic and I didn't realize how big of a deal it was.

Come to find out, it was a really big deal. No one wanted to work with me now, including Funny as Hell. I was embarrassed by what I had done. I only wanted to tell jokes and get noticed. I never meant to disrespect the profession I'd come to love in a short period of time. The fact remained that I'd committed those offenses against fellow comedians. People had worked hard on writing those jokes, and they were their property. For that offense I was truly sorry, and I didn't deserve to be on stage anymore. I didn't deserve to ever call myself a comedian. I dishonorably walked away from comedy, vowing to never return.

Politics Unusual

I felt terrible about what I'd done. Throughout my craziness on stage, I hadn't paid attention to all the people who had walked away from me. Turner Smith had cut me off. Denise Strong had distanced herself from me. My daughter wanted nothing to do with me. Even my wife was second-guessing her commitment because of my behavior. I was beginning to realize that the one thing that made me go crazy was synthetic weed. Once I smoked it, I behaved outrageously. It was rotting my brain and I had to stop. At one time, I'd felt I had to smoke it to perform on stage, and since I'd quit performing, it was the only thing that gave me the high I couldn't get from being on stage. So I kept on smoking it.

The one person who hadn't turned his back on me was Stanley Vegetarian. He knew that I had time on my hands, and he wanted me to come and work on a political campaign with him. He was running for county prosecutor. He was also someone who believed in second chances for people who changed their lives around. Look at how he believed in me.

"Mr. King, I want to hire you as my campaign manager."

"Why would you want to do such a foolish thing? I don't know anything about politics."

"So what?"

"Come on, Stanley, think. Everybody in this town knows me as a criminal and crazy comedian. The only person who knows I have changed my life around is you. That's going to hurt you in the election."

"Why the hell are you always worried about what people think? You're a changed man. Who cares if people don't vote for me because of who you were fourteen years ago? It's good if I don't get their vote, because I don't want it."

"But I could be the reason you lose."

"So what? If I lose, then I lose with my boy."

I couldn't believe Stanley had that much trust in me. If I did this, I had to do it right. We formulated a team to gather enough signatures to get Stanley on the ballot. His opponent was a former judge who was super rich, super connected, and a member of the "Good-Old-Boys Club." It was an uphill battle without those factors, but facing off against color lines and deep pockets made it nearly impossible to compete.

Pardon Me, Counselor

Election night was somber. We lost by a landslide, but we sure did have a lot of fun doing it. The election season not only served as a loss for Stanley, but it was also a loss for Governor Tom Freedom. He had been defeated by Johnny Wright and would no longer be in office. That pretty much meant the end of my petition for a pardon. As much as I felt bad about our losses, I truly had faith that the Lord had something better in store for us. In the words of Turner Smith, if the Lord didn't bless us with a victory, then we didn't need it. I put my trust in Him.

Sleeping in the Jungle

I had finally kicked my habit of smoking synthetic weed and began to see life from a sober point of view. Now that I could see clearly, I saw I had done irreparable damage to my reputation, respect, and credibility during my comedy years. The entire time I was high on that stuff, people thought I'd lost my mind. The good thing was that my mind was coming back to me and everyone could see the positive changes. I might have never got on the straight and narrow if it wasn't for Stanley's political campaign. Stanley had once again been an angel by my side, and I didn't know how I would ever repay him.

•••

As I was eating a late breakfast Saturday afternoon at home before I got ready to run errands, Patience started barking hysterically, so I knew someone must be coming to the door.

"Just a minute." As I rushed to open the door, I looked through the peep hole and saw it was the mailman.

"I have a certified package for David King."

What now? Certified packages usually meant bad news. Either somebody was suing you or you owed somebody some money. I signed for the package and walked into the kitchen. I was skeptical of anything that had a government seal. The moment I opened the envelope, I lost my breath, my left knee buckled, and I fell to the floor.

Elle B. Six

SLEEPING IN THE JUNGLE

GOVERNOR
STATE OF OHIO

WARRANT OF PARDON

I, ▇▇▇▇▇▇ Governor of the State of Ohio, pursuant to Article III, Section 11 of the Ohio Constitution, grant a full pardon to ▇▇▇▇▇▇

After careful and diligent examination of the totality of the materials available to me, I believe that ▇▇▇▇▇▇ has demonstrated that he has been rehabilitated and has assumed the responsibilities of citizenship. A full and unconditional pardon is warranted.

By virtue of the authority vested in me by the constitution of the State of Ohio, I hereby grant a full and absolute pardon to ▇▇▇▇▇▇ for the following convictions:

- ▇▇▇▇▇▇
- ▇▇▇▇▇▇
- ▇▇▇▇▇▇
- ▇▇▇▇▇▇

I have signed this Warrant of Pardon on January 7, 2011, in Columbus, Ohio.

Oh my God! What have You done? This can't be! Did You really do this, Lord? I declared by my faith that You were in control, and that if You didn't bless me with a pardon, then I didn't need it. The moment I took that step of faith, You blessed me! Why do You love me so much, Lord? Who am I? I could hardly contain myself as I rushed out the door, heading for Stanley's office.

"Stanley, I brought you something to read."

As I watched him read, I could see his eyes getting bigger and bigger. "Do you know what this is?"

"Hell yeah, I do. WE DID IT!"

We both screamed and came together for a back-breaking embrace. "Praise God, Mr. King! With this piece of paper, you have your life back. You are fully redeemed. You can do anything in this country that you want to do. You can be a cop, a doctor, a lawyer, anything, even the President if you wanted to."

"Wow, really?"

"Yes! This is an unconditional pardon with all rights restored. This is unprecedented!"

"You know what, then? I want to be a lawyer. That way, I can help people get a second chance like the one I had to fight for. If people want to change their lives around, they should have a chance at redemption also."

"That sounds like a plan to me."

"Are you with me, Stanley?"

"Yes, son, I'm with you! I am so proud of you!"

Order In The Court

This was the day the Lord had made. Stanley hired me as his paralegal so he could teach me everything there was to know about law. No one wanted me to succeed, but that was what pushed me harder. Walking into the Justice Center as a paralegal was one of the most powerful steps I ever took. Sitting in court proceedings as an assistant defense attorney rather than a defendant had people baffled. I was writing defense briefs and closing arguments to defend clients in the same courtroom that had sent me to prison. Stanley and I were such a good team that we never lost a case.

To get into law school, I had to pass the LSAT. Studying for the LSAT was one of the hardest things I ever had to do. I thought I was smart because I'd graduated with a 3.67 GPA when I'd gotten my master's degree, but I couldn't comprehend the LSAT to save my life. The test was so difficult that if you got 50 percent of the answers right then you still passed. The problem was I couldn't get past a 20 percent on any of the practice tests.

The demands of trying to get into law school were taking a toll on me. I was preparing for Stanley's caseloads daily and studying all day, every day. I was once again neglecting my wife, my daughter, and my business for another ambition. It was like I had tunnel vision. I was barely eating or sleeping over the stresses of my workload. I commend anyone who has become a lawyer. It takes more sacrifice than anyone could ever imagine.

BREAKING POINT

Stanley and I were working on a very high-profile murder case. I slept and ate this case, because there was so much riding on it. When I analyzed the evidence and put everything together to mount a proper defense, I realized this guy was guilty as sin. I had never been so sure of someone's guilt in my life. This was a bad guy. He'd killed multiple people in the most gruesome ways imaginable. My conscience would bother me so badly if this guy got off.

"Stanley, this guy is guilty as hell."

"Oh, I know he's guilty."

"What do you mean? Why didn't you tell me?"

"I didn't tell you because all my clients are innocent when they pay me."

"Why do you want to take this guy's case if you know he's guilty?"

"Listen, you might as well get over that shit. Most people who hire a defense attorney are guilty. Very few are innocent. Our mission is to make the guilty appear innocent whether they are or not. That's how you and I make a living. In fact, the better you are at making the guiltiest people appear innocent, the better your practice will be."

"Damn, Stanley. Why don't you tell me how you really feel?"

As we both busted out laughing, I knew there was something about becoming a defense lawyer that gave me the creeps, but I had to suppress my feelings because we had a trial about to start. I really didn't like the defendant, but his life was in our hands. We had to try to give him the best defense we could, but for the first time, I was rooting against us.

During the trial, it was my job to watch the jury. In the opening arguments, I wrote a speech riddled with sarcastic jabs at the prosecution. There was even a hint of humor about the quality of the state's case against Stanley's client. I had to spot any juror who smiled at Stanley while he was talking. I also checked to see if anyone nodded in agreement. I was looking for subtle hints that might give insight into someone leaning our way. After you spotted your jurors, you had a leg up on the prosecution. Every time Stanley got up to speak or cross examine a witness, he would only make eye contact with jurors who agreed with us. That made them feel as if the defense was only talking to them. The more people you had in the deliberating room who were reinforcing the facts you presented, the better chance you had for a favorable verdict. Out of twelve jurors, you only needed one.

•••

Innocent of all charges. I couldn't believe we won. I was happy, Stanley was happy, the defendant was happy, but the victims' families were devastated. Seeing the cries of injustice was more than I could bear. My face was as white as a ghost. All I could think about was what if my dad's killers had had some fast-talking lawyers and they'd been found innocent of the murder of my loved one. The thought that I was a part of freeing the man who'd murdered their loved ones was sickening.

There was no way I could do this for a living. My heart wouldn't allow it. How could I tell Stanley I was not cut out for this? The last thing I wanted to do was disappoint the man who had saved my life in so many ways. I was truly conflicted.

A Father Figure's Love

I owed Stanley the truth, and I prayed he would understand. I hadn't been able to sleep since I'd seen that murderer walk free. *Lord, You know my heart and You know I only want to do Your will. I don't believe that the reason You continue to save my life is to help criminals go free.* However, what if there hadn't been a Stanley there to get me a second chance when I'd been a criminal? I couldn't forget the fact that because of Stanley's expertise, my life had changed. How hypocritical could I be? I was happy when I avoided prison for something I did. I was happy I got a second chance. But now I felt guilty when someone else got a second chance. *Lord, I need You to help me. I need You to lead me.*

We had a long caseload the next day, so I decided to sleep downtown in the office. We had everything on the docket from drug cases to robbery cases. I slowly fell asleep talking on the phone with Kelli before she told me how much she loved me. I snuggled up on the couch in Stanley's office and drifted off to sleep.

I was jolted awake at the sight of a bright light being turned on.

"Rise and shine, Mr. King."

"Hey, what's up, Stanley?" I gave a huge yawn.

"Mr. King, I know you just woke up, but you look tired."

Unable to formulate a response, I gave him a stare.

"You know, there are some people who are cut out for this type of life, but I don't think that you're one of them."

"Don't start tripping, Stanley. I'm good."

"No, you're not, son, and I can see it in your eyes. The same way I saw it in your eyes when we ended that murder trial. I know you look up to me, but this is my life. It's not for everybody. It's a constant grind, and it does involve compromising your morals. I wrestled with it when I first started out, but now I'm desensitized."

As my eyes welled with tears, all I could say was, "I just don't want to let you down."

"You're not letting me down. You have to do what God put you on this earth to do. Don't worry about letting me down. Worry about letting Him down."

We stood together in his office, hugged, and smiled. "We sure did make a hell of a team, didn't we?"

"We sure did, son. We sure did!"

Sleeping in the Jungle

Judge For Yourself

It had only been six months since I'd stopped working with Stanley, and I couldn't believe how much time I had on my hands. I had time for everything and everybody. My finances were looking up as well. I'd had very little time to spend any money when my face was buried in law books. Things were better in a major way.

Just as I was beginning to get comfortable, I receive an unexpected call. "Hello?"

"Brother King."

"If it isn't Stanley Vegetarian. To what do I owe the pleasure, sir?"

"Well, Mr. King, this is duty calling again."

"Duty?"

"Yes, sir, duty! It seems there is a vacancy in our municipal courts, and I want to try to make another run for public office. I realize we led an unsuccessful campaign in the past, but I believe we have a real chance of winning this one. If you have time on your hands, I would love for you to join my campaign staff."

"I would be honored to join your staff, sir. I hope you are prepared to win, because I truly believe this is your time. Let me know where you need me."

"I knew I could count on you, Mr. King. Let's go win this race."

Here we go again!

Lord, please bless Stanley. I would love to see him serve his country in a way that delivered justice for those who were to be judged. If there was anyone in the world who would be fair and impartial, it was Stanley. He would be fair but firm, and if he saw someone who had potential, he would surely give them the second chance they needed. First thing's first, we had to get him elected.

Elle B. Six

•••

Being on the campaign trail with my man Stanley brought back great memories. I always considered myself to be the comedian of the team, but he was just as funny as I was. I handled his speech writing and public appearances. We had endorsements from the veteran's association as well as the police union. Our only concern was voter turnout, because Stanley wasn't well known outside of his law practice. I prayed hard for a successful campaign. Stanley was like my father, and seeing him still hustling as a defense attorney at the age of sixty-eight was taking its toll on me. A victory could change things for the better. He would have the best health insurance, a stable wage, and the best retirement benefits. Outside of the monetary benefits, it was also his dream.

God, if I have any faith capital stored up with You, can I please cash in for Stanley? Thank You for allowing him to achieve his dream.

•••

Election day was intense. We made our final appearances at a few polling stations, but things were not looking good. The latest polling had Stanley's opponent winning by a landslide. With all the forecasts and predictions flying around, I couldn't let that enter my mind. There was only one who was not bound by polls and predictions, and that was the Almighty, and I was putting my faith on His polls.

The first preliminary results were coming in, and as most predicted, we were well behind. With 30 percent of the vote reporting, we were down by 10,000 votes. As 60 percent entered, we were still well behind, but we closed the gap to just 5,000 votes. Ninety percent of the vote came in, and the news reported the race was too close to call. There was only a 600-vote difference between the candidates with one of our best districts left to report. It was shaky, because our opponent had spent a lot of money in that area. Even if we split the vote evenly, we would still lose. We had to win this precinct convincingly. We just had to.

With 100 percent of the vote entered, the projected winner for municipal court judge was Stanley Vegetarian. WE DID IT!

Stanley had the look of pure disbelief on his face, but I was looking for the champagne. I busted open a bottle with a loud popping sound, and I toasted the newest member of the municipal courts. Cheers to my man, Stanley. Thank You, God!

Blacker Than Black

There were times in my life when I was young and naïve. I was not really that young anymore, but I still could have a degree of naïveté. Because I had moved out of the hood and no longer involved myself with hood business, people had begun to speculate why I spent so much time at the Justice Center. It seemed that working on Stanley's prosecutor and judge campaigns, coupled with working inside courtrooms, qualified me as a snitch. *I swear, my people sure can be ignorant at times.* Stanley was a defense attorney. We were inside courtrooms keeping people out of jail, not putting people in jail. I'd worked my butt off to turn my life around, and working with Stanley had been one of the greatest experiences of my life. Without him, I didn't know where I would be.

A snitch was the lowest form of human being. It broke my heart to know anyone thought I could ever be involved with something like that. I guess it could look suspicious. I was a former drug dealer working in courtrooms who'd just gotten a pardon from the governor and was now working on political campaigns. This didn't sound like anything I'd ever heard of when I was in the hood either. I guess I could understand how someone could assume that and spread it around, but it was still unfair. I was not going to worry my head about it, because I was working under God. When you were the first to ever do something, you couldn't expect people to understand, and I was not in the explaining business.

• • •

It had been nearly fifteen years, but finally my man Black was home on parole. I couldn't wait to see him. He had been out of jail for nearly four months, but we had been largely out of touch. I could understand his distance, because it had to be hard getting reacclimated to the hood after being gone so long. One thing that was certainly different about him was his conversion to Islam. Like most black men who spent long periods of time in jail, Islam was both a shield of comfort as well as a shield of protection on the inside. Although we had been apart for so long, the love was still there. I wished there were some crazy amount of cash I had stored up to give him, but that wasn't the case. However, I was not arriving completely empty-handed. I had $10,000 for him, and I couldn't wait to see his face when I dropped it in his lap. I wasn't sure what his plans were for the future, but it sure would be good to have him back in my life.

I walked into a local restaurant that specialized in Islamic food. The walls were all red and hosted cultural posters and pictures of influential figures. There was a small window with light glaring through the inch-thick bulletproof glass where you could place a food order, and a bulletproof winding turnstile to retrieve your food. In the lobby were two black tables with four white chairs. Sitting in one of the chairs was a face I hardly recognized. You could tell it was Black, but you might have second-guessed because of his huge beard. "What's up, big bro?"

"What's up, lil' homey? You look shorter than I remember." He cracked a smile.

"That's funny, you are definitely just as black as I remember. Over here looking like a dark-skinned Bin Laden."

We both broke into laughter and locked each other with a tight bro hug. This was the first time I'd seen my big brother in more than a decade.

"Let's get something to eat and catch up on life."

After eating and talking for what seemed like hours, Black looked as if we had let the time get away from us. "Yo, we gotta wrap this up. I got dropped off up here so I need you to give me a ride. Let's make a quick stop over at my girl's house before you take me home."

"You just got home and you already chasing tail. I thought you were supposed to be religious."

He cracked the biggest smile. "I am religious, but you don't have to be a fanatic."

We laughed as we exited the restaurant and headed to my car. We drove to a house I didn't recognize, and he got out of the car and went inside. He was gone for quite a while, and just as I was beginning to get impatient, he came to the door and waved me inside. He must've wanted me to meet his new flame, but I had to get my appearance together before I met someone for the first time. I took a quick look in the mirror, fixed my face, slapped on cologne, and adjusted my clothing. I walked up on the porch to find the door slightly ajar.

"Hello?" I said in my cool but friendly voice.

As I took a few steps forward, looking around in confusion, I began to let out a second hello when I heard a familiar click-click sound behind me.

"Oh my God." Although it was completely out of place, I knew the sound of a gun being cocked. I didn't want to turn around, but the

Sleeping in the Jungle

door slamming closed prompted me to turn. I began to rotate with my hands raised in the air so I didn't represent a threat.

Black stood there with a shiny silver gun pointed directly at my head.

"What's up, big bro?" My chest was heaving to take breaths, gripped with fear. He didn't say a word as he focused the gun to correct his sight down the barrel. "So, they sent you, huh?" I asked as things were becoming clear that this was a hit. I could see that his eyes were welling with tears.

"FUCK! I can't do it." He swung the gun down in disgust.

My face had to show my anger, fear, and confusion, because I felt my forehead and eyes tighten. "Why would you want to do something like this, bro?"

"I don't know what you been doing since I been gone, but somebody really don't like you. I haven't seen you in fifteen years, and for the money they threw at me, I was really tempted to do it. But looking at you, bro, I remembered we are family and there is no way I can harm you."

Untouched and unmoved by his reversal, I tried to pry as much information as I could get out of him before finding a way to get the hell outta there. "So how much they paying you to kill the son you practically raised?"

"Fifty thousand, but the people who hired me are getting paid more than that. That's why I said somebody really don't like you."

As my tears grew fuller, I refused to let a single one fall. I was too fucking angry to cry. "You know what? If it was God's will that I lose my life today, I trust Him and accept it, but if He's giving me a choice, my choice is to stay and achieve the destiny He put in my heart. On the contrary, if I had to choose the person who would take my life, I guess it would have to be you, bro, because I love you."

"I told you I'm not going to hurt you." He began to walk toward me with his arms extended as if he wanted a hug. With every step he took, I moved a step back with my palm extended forward.

"If you say you can't go through with it then I can leave, right?"

"Yes, you can leave, but—" Before he could finish the sentence, I already had my hand on the lock. "Come on, bro. Can you wait a minute?"

I opened the interior door and ran through the screen door as if it wasn't there.

I heard him yelling from the porch, "I'm sorry. I'm sorry, bro. I'm sorry!"

I jumped into my car and raced down the street. Speeding down street after street, I had so many questions racing through my head. *What the hell just happened? What was that really about? Who in the world wants to kill me that badly?* But the questions that burned in my head the most were: *What made Black unable to kill me? Was it that he couldn't go through with it because he remembered his love for me, or did God stop him? Could it be that the Lord had stepped in to save my life again? Why would God want anything to do with me?* My life had been a mess, and on top of that, I had a hunger for vengeance.

Outta There

It seemed like somebody really wanted me dead—to try to use my own man to take me out. They also seemed to want me so badly that they were paying a ridiculous amount of money to make it happen.

I knew people who would take out a whole area code for that kind of money. I knew some killers of my own, and they would put in work for a hell of a lot less than what these guys were paying. However, retaliation was something that I could never do. I served a God who had the ability to step in and save me from harm, so I didn't need protection from men. Once again, the Lord intervened when I was about to be hurt. Why would I jeopardize my favor with the Almighty by doing something stupid like having someone else hurt? It was my choice to just walk in faith and rely on the protection He has shown me my whole life.

Once I prayed about my experience, I realized God may have used Black's attempt as a tool to warn me of the danger that could be around any corner. I needed to get out of town, but that was easier said than done. The last thing I was going to do was tell Kelli what happened. She had a flourishing career and shouldn't have her life dictated by any of this street crap.

No sooner than I knew I had to get out of town did Kelli walk in with a proposal. "David, you're not going to believe this, but I got offered a promotion at my job. The only catch is that we would have to move to Philadelphia. I know you don't want to go, but—"

I instantly cut her off. "You're kidding. Get out of here?"

"Look, I know we probably can't take it because of your business but..."

"No, don't worry about the business. I want to support you. I can pay someone to manage my properties for me, and we can move on to the next chapter."

"Really?"

"Of course."

"Oh my God, I think we're moving to Philly then."

"Congratulations, baby. We are out of here."

What a stroke of luck. The Lord was getting us out of here before I'd even had a chance to pray about it. He never ceased to amaze me. Kelli was promoted to Sales Manager for Exton Pharmaceuticals. It was an unbelievable opportunity with a wide territory. She was responsible for New York, New Jersey, Virginia, Maryland, and Pennsylvania. She had to spend a lot of time on the road, and she was scared to drive so much by herself, so I volunteered to drive her to appointments that were farther away.

Elle B. Six

We spent so much time on the open road that we were never in the same place too long. I still couldn't believe she had landed a job that made us virtually invisible at a time when I really needed to disappear. I was out of sight and all over the East Coast. I was alive and safe, but I felt empty inside. I didn't know what to do. I didn't know what was missing.

D-Press-Shun

For some reason, the hardest thing for me to do was get out of bed. Showering took an Act of Congress. I had lost my feeling of safety and security. One of the things I missed the most was the ability to perform on stage. Every night when I would fall asleep, I could hear the crowd laughing. I could hear applause. I could feel the affirmation of a well-placed punchline at the end of a joke.

Boy, I'd really made a mess of things. I balked at people who looked up to me. I balked at people who thought I was special. I felt like my mom, dad, and even God was wrong about me. I was nothing. I was a nobody. Four college degrees and a lifetime of chasing greatness, and I hated myself. I rarely tended to my business because I felt like people were out to get me everywhere. My business was suffering. I lost my grip with reality, and one of the few men I loved like a father had tried to kill me. What did I have to live for? I wished Black had killed me that day and put me out of my misery. Hey, maybe that was it. Maybe my time on this earth was up.

"IS THAT WHAT YOU'RE TRYING TO TELL ME, LORD? SHOULD I BOW OUT OF THIS WORLD GRACEFULLY AND JOIN YOU? WHAT DO YOU WANT FROM ME? ANSWER ME. ANSWER ME."

Why would the Lord waste His time answering someone who had

strayed as far as I had? I said I had my faith in Him, but I feared everything and everyone. I had a wife and child who could easily get caught up in the danger meant for me. It was time I freed the people I loved from the misery of having me in their lives. My death could be just the blessing they needed to move on. I knew what I could do. I could take out a large life insurance policy on myself and let fate deal with the rest. This would ensure my family's financial security and free me from this world at the same time.

Heavenly Plan

It had been six months and I was still alive, but it wasn't by accident. Although I put this plan into place, I seemed to be petrified of how the end would come. I was extremely paranoid. I never accepted an invitation from anybody, and I never let anyone know where I was going to be. When I came into the city, I was in disguise, and I was usually in and out in the matter of a day. For a person who wanted to die, I seemed to be doing everything in the world imaginable to avoid it. I had nightmares all the time about how the end would come and who would do the killing. I very seldom traveled with Kelli anymore because I didn't want her to become a casualty of my stupidity.

Whenever there was danger, the Lord always warned me. Whenever I felt the slightest discomfort, I was out of there. I couldn't keep living like this, but my biggest fear was that death would hurt. What if my killer was not very good and they messed me up but I didn't die? What if I got paralyzed or something? What if I got maimed really badly and was forced to live with a disability? I just couldn't leave my homecoming in the hands of wannabe killers. I was going to have to take care of it myself.

Suicide was out of the question, because my family would not receive an insurance payout. How could I die without having to be shot, stabbed, or blown up? I had to make it look accidental, but I also wanted to do it without pain. What good was a person's life when his only sources of love were his wife and his dog? Kelli and Patience were all I had in this world, and they would be better off without me.

I was never happier than the moment I developed a divine idea. It took some deep thinking, but I had finally figured out a way for me to take my life pain-free while making it look like an accident. Thank the Lord for helping me through, and I would be with Him soon.

I left West Philadelphia with an ounce of the finest marijuana that money could buy. The fine herb would not just serve as a celebration for my homecoming: it was a crucial part of my plan. The next time Kelli went on a business trip, I was going to pull my car into the garage, close the door, leaving the car running, and smoke until I fell into a deep eternal sleep. When the police found my body, they would think I was in the car getting high and had failed to realize the danger of the toxic fumes. I was glad I didn't have to deal with this life anymore. I was ready for whatever happened next.

Patience Is A Virtue

Watching as Kelli prepared for her business trip was bittersweet. God had truly blessed me with the most beautiful wife any man could ever ask for. I prayed she found happiness beyond the tragedy of losing me. I asked the Lord to keep her happy and bring the perfect man into her life. Someone who would love and appreciate her as much as I did. She was an angel, and I would miss her so much. *Take care, princess, and may God love and keep you forever!*

I sat on the edge of the bed with my little dog Patience, and I couldn't help thinking about all the places I'd gone wrong. All the people I had disappointed. Why had the Lord spared my life so many times? Tears welled up in my eyes and began to flow like a faucet.

"Why have You forsaken me, Lord? Why have You burdened me with so much sorrow?" I screamed as the pain of my actions took root. This was it and I knew it. *It's time to let Your will be done.*

I tried to put myself back together so I could get things in motion, and I felt a subtle touch against my cheeks that were soaking wet from crying. I looked up to see Patience standing up on my leg and slowly licking my tears. He was so small that his tongue was only the size of a penny, but it broke me from my hysteria for a brief second.

"Go on, boy. Go lay down." I gazed into his eyes and he gazed into mine. He refused to obey my order and slowly began to lick away more tears again. Patience was ten years old. He was extremely obedient, and it was out of his character not to obey a command.

I said more sternly, "Go on, boy. Go lay down now." I arose from

Sleeping in the Jungle

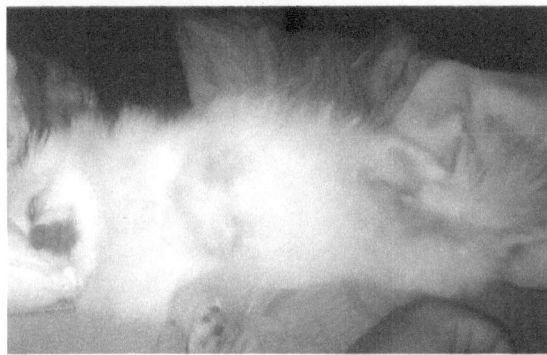

the bed so that I could finish what I started. I turned to Patience. "I love you, good boy. Take care of your mommy for me, and don't give her any trouble." I was bawling while I rubbed his stomach. "I will always love you, good boy."

I rose to an upright position, took a step over to pick up my bag of weed, and looked over to see Patience taking a dump right in the middle of the bed. "What the hell are you doing? Why didn't you tell me you had to use the bathroom?"

I quickly picked him up and rushed him outside. Patience had been housebroken since he was a year old. He hadn't used the bathroom in the house in years, let alone on my bed. In my hysteria, I didn't realize he hadn't gone out all day. I had spent so much time talking about how nobody loved me or needed me except Kelli and Patience that I'd never realized maybe that was enough.

If I was gone, who was going to make sure my good boy pee-peed outside while Kelli was working? Who was going to drive my wife around the East Coast? Who was going to make Patience's food like he liked it with a few pieces of shredded cheese on top? Who was going to cook for my beautiful wife? Make the best love to her? Maybe I did have purpose in this world. Maybe the Lord has just answered the question I'd been asking. Who was I?

New Lease

It was funny how God could use something as small as a dog to be a messenger. I had spilled the whole gallon of milk throughout my battles with depression and it was not like I could just put the milk back in the jug. I couldn't just call up my enemies and say, "Hey, I was just bullshitting." I couldn't just call up people I'd publicly disrespected and say, "My bad." I had to try to make things right, but I had no idea what that would even look like. What I did know was that I had pissed a lot of people off, but there was nothing I could do about it. I just had to lay low and hope things blew over.

•••

For the next couple of years, I kept my nose clean and was beginning to put my business back together. I purchased seven more properties in my hometown and was able to creep back and forth in town to make sure the renovations were going according to plan. With thirty-seven total properties in my portfolio, I was clearing enough profits to secure my family's future. Fear was one of the tools that the devil used to knock you off your path, so I decided to return to my hometown to make things right. I had the Lord's protection, and He and I were a majority. Kelli, Patience, and I were headed home.

Kelli and I found the most beautiful patch of land to build a house on just south of the city, a 5,000-square-foot masterpiece surrounded by a ravine and hundreds of trees. It was completely secluded with only one neighbor. I had never felt more confident about life. I would be close to my business and maybe I could even repair my relationship with my daughter. There was only prosperity ahead, and things were looking up.

The Southern Novelists

Kelli had taken a position at a prominent financial company as a director of sales. It would take me a couple of years to finish building my house the way I wanted it. A couple of years would also give Kelli enough time to get comfortable in her new career. While I found the right contractors and scheduled renovations, I needed something to occupy my time. My life had been such a roller coaster that I wanted to look into writing an autobiography. Telling my story properly would take a lot of work, considering I'd never written a book before. My plan for occupying my time began with writing a story of triumph. I purchased myself a laptop and quickly began to write about my experiences.

After a year of writing, I saw that I was putting together quite a story. Writing about my life had a sobering effect and opened a lot of old wounds. There were so many things that happened in my life that I would like to forget about, but to tell where you were going, you have to tell where you've been. It was teaching me a real lesson about who I really was: a blessed man.

Elle B. Six

Now that I was becoming serious about writing my story, I needed professional assistance. There was a writers' group that met at the local library every month, and they helped writers develop their stories. I didn't know what to expect from the group, but I knew I needed them. If I could find a way to tell my story properly, it could turn out to be something that might help someone else. I walked in with the determination to join the group no matter the cost. The Lord hadn't given me this unique story to keep to myself. He wanted me to use it to inspire someone.

I walked into the meeting and got the feeling that I may have come to the wrong place. The entire group was made up of Caucasian senior citizens. It put me in the mind of when someone walked into a room and a record scratched. After an awkward stare for a few seconds, I was quickly welcomed by the group's leader, Ms. Sassy Jordan. Sassy stood at about 5'2". She had a head full of perfectly curled gray hair, and she walked with a cane. She had run the group for more than forty years and had developed spectacular writers.

"Welcome to the Southern Novelists, and thank you so much for coming. We have a great meeting prepared for us today, so you picked the right day to join us. Please come on in and have a seat."

When I say that the group welcomed me with open arms, that would be an understatement. I absolutely loved my new friends, and they loved me too. We were not just a writers' group: we became a family. Before each meeting, we met for dinner at a local diner just to catch up with current events. We also gathered in small groups to attend book signing events. Could you imagine a thirty-five-year-old muscular black man sitting at a book signing with five Caucasian ladies in their sixties and seventies? People stared sometimes but we didn't care. We were just doing our own thing!

Sleeping in the Jungle

• • •

As we were concluding another successful monthly writers' meeting, I decided to confide in Sassy about my desire to be a comedic writer as well as a dramatic writer. The one thing I loved about Sassy was that she did not sugarcoat what she had to say. If you wanted politically correct, the Southern Novelists was not the group for you.

"Hey, Sassy, what do you think about me taking a crack at comedy writing after I made a complete fool of myself years ago?"

"Look kid, who cares about what anyone thinks? This is about you. If you want it, you have to go get it. You can use the same writing principles I taught you for your book to do your comedy. Until you get serious about writing and start bringing in material for us to see, I'm not going to keep giving you these pep talks."

I absolutely loved that woman! She reminded me so much of my mom. She was tough and didn't take any crap. Whoever named her Sassy knew what they were doing.

One of my favorite TV shows was *The Chappelle Show*. It was a controversial sketch comedy series that walked the line of being offensive. They pushed political correctness to its breaking point. Once I got my first taste of the show, I knew I could write one like that. Maybe something like that would be my comedic outlet. I vowed I would never return to doing stand-up comedy because I was too ashamed, but maybe sketch comedy would be my calling.

I began using Sassy's writing principles to write some of the craziest comedy sketches. Of course, I thought it was good enough for the next level, but if I was unproven, how would I ever know? I really needed to find someone to help me film my sketches, but I didn't want to reach out to anyone in town, because nobody knew I was living back in Ohio. What was I going to do? I woke up every night writing new ideas and sketches, but it wouldn't make a difference if no one ever got to see them. *Lord, I need Your help once again. If this is truly what You want me to do with my life, can You please show me how to make it happen?*

Shifting Gears

This month's writers' meeting was going to be crazy. It was the first meeting where I was going to introduce my comedic writing to the entire group. If I could make elderly white people laugh with sketches, I knew I had a recipe for mass appeal. I could tell that the meeting was going to be different in more ways than one. There were two young men there who were identical twins and couldn't be more than nineteen. They were white kids with red hair and faces full of freckles. If I was out of place at the age of thirty-five, then they were definitely in the wrong place.

"Hello, gentlemen. How are you? Welcome to our writers' group. My name is David."

"Hi, David. I'm John, and this is Joseph and our mom Janine."

"It is a pleasure to meet you all. Are you all writers?"

"Actually, no. We're filmmakers. We just completed our first film and we are struggling to find our next thing. So, I guess we are just filmmakers looking for stories."

"Wow, guys, you're not going to believe this, but I have stories that are looking for filmmakers, so that means you definitely came to the right place. Let's exchange numbers and work on filming some of the scripts I have written!"

"That sounds great! We came looking for a match but we never thought we would find someone this fast."

Sleeping in the Jungle

What a blessing. Out of the clear blue sky, these young men appeared in my life after I'd specifically prayed for them. The boys had completed their first film that had some award-winning success for a student film, but you could tell it was shot on low-budget equipment. I had the grandest idea. I was going to buy top-of-the-line filming equipment so they would be able to drastically upgrade the quality of their productions. That way, when we began working together, we could produce TV-quality comedy scenes.

The amazing thing about my new team was that it wasn't just two brothers, there were three. John and Joseph had a younger brother named Israel. He was only fifteen but was smarter than all of us. He was the sound guy. I had a hard time believing that three teenage boys could be so industrious. Their parents had raised these young men the right way, and it showed. It also didn't escape me that all the boys' names were from the Bible. They had been just as much of a blessing to me as I was to them. I couldn't wait until they saw the new equipment I'd bought for them.

•••

As the equipment began to arrive, I couldn't believe how excited the boys were. They were like small kids on Christmas morning. High-definition cameras, hard drives, LED lighting kits and high-quality sound equipment. Every package the boys opened was a new celebration. I knew they would be happy, but I didn't know they would be that happy. I just wanted to make sure that if we did it, we did it right.

Now that we had the equipment, it was time to get to work. I gave the boys access to my computer so they could study the comedy sketches and start scouting for shooting locations. While we were strolling through my files, we came across the opening for my book called *Sleeping in the Jungle*. As they read through the words, their eyes got wider and wider.

"Hey, guys, this story is awesome! David, do you think we could make this into a short film?"

"A short film? What in the world is that?"

"Come on, David. You don't know what a short film is? They're made all the time. Our first film was a short film that was only twenty-four minutes."

"I don't know, guys. You are supposed to be scouting locations to shoot these comedy sketches, and you come up with a short film. We might have to put that on hold."

"Please, David," they pleaded. "Okay, don't answer us yet. Come with us to the Sundance Short Film Festival and then let us know what you think."

"Okay, I don't see the harm in that. We'll go."

I went to the festival and completely fell in love with short film. With every film that we saw at Sundance, more ideas began to flow through my head. I'd started out saying the short films would have to wait until we finished with the comedy sketches, but it was the comedy sketches that would have to wait. Me and my boys were about to make a movie.

SLEEPING IN THE JUNGLE

I had no experience making movies, but my boys had done it before. However, because it was my story, I had to take the lead. *Where do I begin? How do I set it up? Who will my actors be?* Making a movie was not a simple task, especially if I wanted to make it something special. You never get a second opportunity to make a first impression, and it was going to be the first time I introduced myself as a filmmaker.

To get inspiration I decided to go to the movies. The N.W.A. biopic *Straight Outta Compton* was coming out about the hip-hop supergroup. Right there in the movie theater, I felt the biggest sense of inspiration. The character playing Ice Cube was sitting in front of a computer. His wife walked in and asked Ice Cube how the movie was coming along. He said great and mouthed the words, *You got knocked the fuck out.*

That was it! To make a movie, you took it scene by scene and line by line. I came here looking for inspiration, and because Ice Cube was my source of inspiration, it was apparent you'd have no idea who the Lord would use to get you the information you needed.

I wrote the film, but I had no idea if it was any good. The only thing that made me feel like it had potential was that everyone who read it started to cry. If the film could make you cry, it had impact. The boys were so excited to make it that they could hardly wait to get started. They hired all their friends as the cast. I even had Kelli in the film. I was going to play my father, but the only character who was proving to be difficult to find was one who would play me. We had several young men audition, but none of them blew me away. Once we filled the role, we could get started, but we were having no luck.

I recruited a young man named Christopher from a local college nearby. Christopher was masterful at stage performances, so he would be able to make a natural transition to film. He was a light-skinned kid with curly hair and very well spoken. If he wasn't so tall, he could really pass for my son. He was a natural at catching the emotions of each scene.

For my first film production, it was really turning out to be nice. We found the perfect jungle gym for Christopher to sleep in. We also found the perfect store to film in front of. It was crazy, seeing my life play out on camera. Some scenes reflected the darkest periods of my life and were very difficult to direct without becoming emotional. Reenacting the time I'd slept in the jungle gym and the events that led to my father's murder were terrifying. It would also be the first time I'd revealed the fact that it could have been my fault my dad had been murdered. It was more drama than I could take. I teared up at every scene, and my heart pumped faster as I had to relive the horror of how I'd felt back then.

Elle B. Six

SLEEPING IN THE JUNGLE
BASED ON A TRUE STORY

WINNER
NEW YORK CITY IDEPENDENT FILM AWARDS
BEST SHORT FILM 2017

OFFICIAL SELECTION
41st CLEVELAND INTERNATIONAL
FILM FESTIVAL

WINNER
NORTHEAST OHIO INTERNATIONAL FILM FESTIVAL
BEST SHORT FILM 2017

WINNER
VERMILION FILM FESTIVAL
BEST SHORT FILM 2017

OFFICIAL SELECTION
HAMILTON MUSIC & FILM AWARDS 2017

OFFICIAL SELECTION
SCOUT FILM FESTIVAL 2017

OFFICIAL SELECTION
NORTH BY NORTHWEST FILM FESTIVAL 2017

OFFICIAL SELECTION
FILM FORUM ON THE LAKE 2017

Look out the Window

I had a vacancy in one of my properties that was very easy to rent, a three-bedroom duplex with a large living room and dining room. I'd placed an ad on Craigslist and had a dozen families who were interested. My only challenge would be choosing the best tenant for the property. I scheduled the interviews forty-five minutes apart so I wouldn't have any overlap from the previous appointment. I couldn't wait to get this over with so I could remove my phone number from the internet. Whenever I placed an ad, I got some of the craziest calls in the world.

My first interview was with a girl who had two children. She said she had first month's rent and security deposit, but I wanted to know her rental history more than I wanted her money. Her money wouldn't do me any good if I never received another dollar from her after she moved in. Another thing to watch for was serial movers. If the tenant couldn't stay in one place long term, the odds were that they weren't stable.

The girl was supposed to meet me at noon, and she was fifteen minutes late, so that was a bad sign. Punctuality was important if you were trying to get a landlord to turn their property over to you. I decided to put in a call.

"Hello?"

"Yes, hello ma'am. This is the landlord calling that you were scheduled to meet. I just wanted to see if you were on your way, or do you need to reschedule?"

"Oh no, I'm outside right now in a little blue car. I'm not sure where I should come in, though."

"Okay, great. Stay there, and I will come down to get you."

As soon as I took a step toward the door, I heard a strong voice in my head say, *Don't go out there. Look out the window.*

I stopped, and my heart began to beat really fast. I started to overrule the feeling, but for some reason it was crippling. Every step I tried to take, my legs felt like they weighed a ton. I stepped over to the window, looked out and instantly froze. There was a man standing by the side of the house holding a gun. I closed the curtain and ran to the other side of the house, and there was another man there with a gun. Looking out the back, I saw three more. *What the hell is this shit?* Thinking on my toes, I quickly called 911.

"Nine-one-one, how may I help you?"

"Yes, ma'am, I was meeting a potential tenant from Craigslist and there are men standing around the house with guns. I think it could be a robbery or worse. I need help, ma'am, fast."

"Okay, stay on the line with me and I'm sending help."

I hoped they would show up to catch these guys in the act. I didn't know what they wanted—to rob me or kill me—but I planned on getting out of there. I heard a quick beep on the phone, and I recognized it was the girl I was supposed to meet. I'd almost forgotten about her. I had to warn her before she got hurt, so I clicked over and peeked out the window.

"Hello?" she said.

"Yes, I'm sorry I can't come out to meet you. There are some guys outside, and they look like they're up to no good. You might want to leave so you don't get hurt."

As soon as I clicked back over to the 911 operator, I saw the prospective tenant give a signal to the thugs, pull away rapidly, and all the men took off running. *Oh my God, they were together.* It was a setup. As soon as the police came, I made my way outside. They escorted me to the freeway safely and told me to get out of the neighborhood. Yeah, I was going to get out of the neighborhood, all right. In more ways than one.

Gone Too Soon

I couldn't believe there had been another attempt on my life. I didn't know if it was just a random Craigslist setup for a robbery or someone from my past. Either way, I was shaken to my core. I wanted to run a successful business, but I didn't want to die doing it. This was proving to be more than I could stand. I had a family who needed me. I had to find a safer way to make a living. The one thing I couldn't deny was the Lord's protection. He'd clearly told me there was danger outside. When I'd tried to overrule the feeling, He'd stopped my legs from being able to move. What was it about me that the Lord deemed it a priority to save me from danger? People die every day. Why were the signs so clear to me?

I felt danger everywhere I went in Cleveland. It was clear that this was not the place for me. I loved the city more than I could describe, but the city did not love me back. I'd made a mistake by trying to move back there. I felt the Lord was trying to tell me I had nothing to prove or make right with my hometown. I was going to stay long enough to sell my new house and make my movie. I would simply hire someone to manage my business, but I had to get out of there. The funny thing was that no one even knew I'd ever moved back so they surely wouldn't notice when I was gone.

I offered Jonesy's little brother Nicky a small part in my movie. He was an ambitious young man who couldn't catch a break. I'd mentored him since he was a little kid, but now he was twenty. He was very tall and athletic and had led my alma matter Tri-C to a basketball championship. He wanted the greatest things out of life, but every time he tried to get ahead, he kept getting knocked down. He had never been in any legal trouble. He always kept a job and attended college faithfully. There was no reason why he couldn't rise and be successful, and hopefully acting in his first movie would give him a new direction.

The phone rang. "Hello?"

The person began to scream incoherently. "THEY GOT EM, BRO. AAAAAAAAAGH."

"Jonesy, is that you?"

There was more screaming and him shouting, "Why?"

"Jonesy, slow down, man. I can hardly understand you."

The phone disconnected.

I couldn't understand him because he was trying to tell me Nicky had just been murdered in broad daylight on the basketball court on East 75th and Kinsman. He'd been shot in the back as he'd stood in the middle of the playground.

The shock of the news had frozen every muscle in my body. I didn't have the strength to maintain a grip on my cell phone as it slipped from my hand and crashed to the floor. How could this happen? A young man with so much promise. Jonesy and his family were devastated. It had gotten to the point where I didn't recognize my hometown anymore. The violence was getting out of control.

•••

Sleeping in the Jungle

The recent uptick in violence had the mayor and city council up in arms. They decided to throw a music concert at Woodhill Park to bring the community together. The event was called "United in the Park" and would be headlined by the mighty O'Jays, a Cleveland-born R&B group that had been successful since the seventies. This was just what the city needed, a free event the whole family could enjoy that would surely change the tone of the crazy summer.

The concert was being held just minutes from where Kelli grew up, and her whole family planned to attend. This was the first time I could remember that there had been an effort like that to bring the community together. Having live entertainment in the local park with free admission was almost unheard of. The police presence was massive, and the barbecue smelled so good. Adults, kids, and pets were all welcome.

What an amazing concert! Everyone thoroughly enjoyed themselves. The police presence was as heavy as I imagined it would be, which gave everyone a sense of security. As soon as the event ended, there was a streaming crowd trying to exit.

Just as the night was nearing perfection, we heard gun shots ring out. My heart felt like it leaped out of my body. "Kelli, what was that?"

"Let's get the hell out of here."

With my adrenaline at its highest level, we headed straight for the car, as there was mass hysteria everywhere. People were running, screaming, and desperately searching for loved ones. *Why couldn't we just have one evening without violence?* This was supposed to be the United in the Park concert, and although the night was hugely successful, it would be known for the events that happened afterward.

Just as we made it back to the car, Kelli's phone rang. It was her mom, and we could barely make out a word she was saying. All we could hear was, "They shot him! Oh my God, they shot him."

Kelli tried to ask "Who?" but she didn't receive a coherent answer.

When you receive a message that says they shot "him" but you don't know who, your mind begins to race. Was it Kelli's father who had been shot? Her brother?

Kelli's face was in pure terror as she saw emergency vehicles arriving on the scene. With everyone trying to run away, it made it extremely difficult to break through the crowd. Once we arrived, we saw Kelli's mom covered in blood and her seventeen-year-old nephew Terrell lying dead on the ground.

With all the hysteria going on, it seemed like the entire earth turned silent. All I could do was stare in disbelief at the totality of what had unfolded. It was more than I could digest; I was completely frozen in the moment. I couldn't scream. I couldn't help. I couldn't even move. I couldn't comprehend what was happening.

Out of all the people we imagined who could be shot, we never thought it would be Terrell. Why would anybody want to hurt him? He was so young. He'd been shot two times in the head and had no chance of survival. How could something like this happen?

There were crowds of people standing around, but no one was willing to say what they'd seen. Police had been everywhere, and a murder had still taken place. Was anyone safe in the hood anymore? First Nicky, now Terrell.

Kelli's family was devastated. This was a new level of grief. This family had been no stranger to loss of life, but this was different. Terrell had had his whole life ahead of him. He'd been a young vibrant high school student who'd stayed to himself. If he was not safe, none of us were.

As I began to process all the devastation, I felt a cramp in the pit of my stomach. Although I had the Lord's protection, it was up to me to recognize the warning signs He sent. Nicky was killed on 75th and Kinsman. My father had lost his life on 83rd and Kinsman. Terrell had just been murdered on 93rd and Kinsman. The next main intersection was 116th and Kinsman. I owned a four-unit apartment building there. It was one of my most profitable rentals. But I felt like the reaper was making its way up the block, and I was scared to death.

Everywhere I looked, I saw death and destruction. I had gotten so paranoid that I didn't even go to my Kinsman property anymore. Kelli was feeling as if her time in Cleveland was over as well. It didn't matter how much we loved that place—when it didn't love you back, you had to move on. It would take us some time to get our affairs in order, but the writing was on the wall.

Casino Effect

My search for someone to take over the management of my real estate portfolio had not worked out well. There wasn't anyone who would do the job with the passion I would do it with. It was almost like the business knew I was leaving, because I was having problems I'd never encountered before. I learned that having a casino within minutes of the inner city was not a good thing for those who couldn't handle the temptation. So many families were negatively affected by the presence of a casino. When a household lost just one paycheck to the slot machines, it could take months to recover. The children were the ones who were affected the most, but no one seemed to see it.

The one thing I noticed the most was that the casinos had taken away the help of the grandparents. There'd been a time when if funds fell short, you could always count on Grandma for assistance. When you had to get school clothes, the grandparents came through. Now, many of the grandparents had succumbed to the gambling bug, and that support had evaporated. It broke my heart when I saw large busloads of elderly people pulling up to the casino, knowing the dire consequences it was having on the children and grandchildren who depended on them so much. When a family lost the electric bill money, the kids suffered. Lose the rent money, and the kids suffer. When the money was gone, Mommy and Daddy were angry and intolerant. Lunch money for kids was suffering, and there was no money for field trips and clothes. The list went on and on.

When a casino listed its monthly profits of $21 million, where did people think that money came from? The increase in violence and desperation could also be attributed to gambling. If you were a drug dealer, your money was your job. If you lost your money to buy drugs, you were unemployed. There was also the fact that drug dealers didn't own the drugs they sold. There was a difference when you lost your money compared to losing someone else's money at the casino. This meant they had to get the money back by any means necessary or they could be killed. If their life was in jeopardy, robberies and murders were going to increase, and the value of life diminished greatly. I had friends in Detroit who said we didn't want casinos in Cleveland. Now I understood what they meant.

There was a family in one of my properties that was particularly hit hard by this scenario. Whenever things were tight throughout the year, income tax time would make up the difference. Unfortunately, the mom got drunk, felt lucky, and lost her entire tax rebate check. Grandma used to step in and help every month because the mom had four kids, but Grandma was down on her luck at the slots as well. The mom was Ms. Cynthia, and she worked nonstop but was still unable to make ends meet. She was shuffling money between utilities and rent, but it was really taking a toll on her. She had become so bitter about her circumstances that she had even become angry with me whenever rent was due. Although I was sympathetic, she was two months behind on rent and I had to evict her. That was what I hated about my profession. Good business practices involved making decisions that would put a mom and four kids out on the street. My conscience was killing me, but rent had to be paid.

I delivered Ms. Cynthia an eviction notice while she was at work, because the last thing I felt like doing was arguing with her. I delivered one to the front door and one in the mailbox.

I was headed out the door when her fifteen-year-old son Markus came running out behind me.

"Excuse me, Mr. David. Can I talk to you for a minute?"

"Sure, son. What's up?"

"Sir, does the notice mean you are putting us out?"

Responding somberly, I said, "I'm afraid so, but I can't speak about this matter with you. I can only speak to your mom."

"Please don't do this, sir!" His eyes filled with tears.

"I'm afraid I can't talk to you about this, son. I'm really sorry."

"Mr. David, this will devastate my mom. She is up crying every night over money. Is there anything I can do to earn some money to help her?"

I was moved by the gesture, because I remembered exactly what it felt like to be desperate to survive. My heart was also moved simply because I saw so much of myself in young Markus. I was fifteen when I'd faced homelessness, and I felt compelled not to put this family in the same situation. "You know what, Markus? Give me that notice back and don't make any mention of this to your mother. I want you to clean the basement and the yard, and we'll call it even on the rent."

"Really?"

"Absolutely."

"Thank you, sir, thank you! I will clean it up right away. Thank you."

I forgave $1,100 worth of rent for about fifty bucks' worth of cleaning.

I felt like I got my money's worth. The desperation in that kid's eyes was very familiar to me. I wanted to show him some of the mercy people had shown me when I was on the streets. It was funny, out of all the evictions I'd done over the years, this was the first time I'd ever considered what the children had to go through. I had some soul searching to do.

White Flag

I couldn't believe what I'd just heard! Ms. Cynthia called me to tell me that Markus had been killed. *How on earth could this happen to that kid? Where did it happen? Who did it?* I had so many questions, but there was so much chaos.

I saw Ms. Cynthia on the news every night crying and asking for justice. The story from the streets was that fifteen-year-old Markus had been attempting to sell drugs on a known gang corner and had been killed for the violation. When I'd seen his desperation, all I saw was myself. He was probably trying to make money to help his mom with rent. All I could remember was the fear on his face when he'd thought they were being evicted. Just the thought of that kid being homeless by my hands was a task I could not handle. Although I didn't feel any guilt or responsibility, I knew this business was not for me anymore. Instead of finding someone to manage it, I had to find someone to purchase it. Time to cash out and move on.

Lord, You know my heart and You know I cannot do this anymore. I am asking You to take this burden off me and allow Your will to be done. It is my only desire to please You, and if You want me to stay and fight I will, but if Your will is for me to go, I need You to get me out of here.

Sleeping in the Jungle

Partial Obedience

The *Sleeping in the Jungle* short film had a significant impact. It won several film festivals and was accepted into dozens more. It was amazing to have that much success on our first film, and we really hadn't known what we were doing. I'd just purchased some camera equipment and we'd hit "record." Considering me and Kelli's desire to move away, I didn't think about my new relationship with John, Joseph, and Israel. Before they'd met me, they'd been filming their movies on regular camera equipment, and now they were using top-of-the-line equipment. If I moved away and took the equipment with me, it would set them back to where they started. I had the desire to help them out, because these kids had been sent to me after I'd prayed for help, so I knew they were from God. I couldn't just leave them hanging.

I decided I needed to pray on it, but I was surprised by the answer. That night I heard God say, "Give them all the equipment." Not out loud, but in my mind. I thought to myself, there was no way I was going to give them all the equipment. I wanted to start a new film production company and I needed that equipment for my new venture. Plus, I'd spent a significant amount of money on it, and I couldn't just give it away. I knew what I could do. I could give them one of the cameras and some lighting to get them started, and that would put them on the path to success.

Riding in my car, there did not seem to be anything to listen to on the local radio, so I turned on my satellite radio to see what was on. Then I got distracted and didn't realize the channel was tuned to a radio preacher I'd never heard of named Pastor O. I had a personal relationship with God, but I didn't listen to preachers or go to church. As I reached toward the radio to search for a new channel, I heard the preacher say something I could not believe.

"If God tells you to do something, then do it. Partial obedience is not obedience. If God tells you to give somebody a ride to church, you are not obeying God fully if you find them a ride to church. There is a reason why He told you to give them a ride. Don't miss out on the great blessings you have in store because you refuse to be obedient to the One who controls it all."

When Pastor O said those words, I knew he was talking to me. God had told me to bless those boys with all the equipment, and that was exactly what I was going to do.

Consider all the things that had to line up for that message to get to me. There had to be nothing on the local radio. I had to turn to satellite radio. The satellite was tuned to a pastor I'd never listened to or heard of. I'd gotten distracted so I wouldn't turn the channel. Once I'd realized what was on, the pastor had to utter the message before my hand had an opportunity to change the channel.

Adding all that up at a time when I wrestled with a direct command from God, I realized the message was not just a message from a radio preacher. It was a message from above.

●●●

Giving the boys the equipment was the highlight of my life. They were so happy and extremely excited for the future. It was both a happy time and a sad one, because I also had to tell them I was looking to move away. Israel was the youngest and the most outspoken. "You can't leave, though, Dave. We are just getting started."

"I know, guys, but it is too difficult to explain."

Then one of the twins told me something I couldn't believe. "You don't understand, David. We prayed for you. We prayed at church one day that we would be able to make movies on high-quality equipment and you just appeared out of nowhere and let us use this great stuff. We prayed we would make movies that made a difference, and your story has also provided that. We say all the time that you were sent to us from God."

Me? Sent from God, really? Didn't they know I'd prayed for them and that they were my angels, not vice versa?

Then I realized we were both doing God's work. That was when I began to flash back. Every time I prayed, ordinary people showed up and blessed me. Turner Smith told me that God had told him to help me. God had also told me to help these boys.

I'd listened to Pastor O every day since I'd first turned on the satellite radio, and one day he said the Lord was using people to do a work in us or using us to do a work in other people.

Was the reason why the Lord had sent so many angels to save me over the years because He wanted to use me to bless others? In the Bible, there were many examples of ordinary people who had the Lord's protection. Was this what I was supposed to do with my life? Keep following the path He'd set for me and be obedient along the way? I had a new lease on life, but I had to figure out what my purpose was, because it couldn't be for me to be engulfed in chaos and violence.

The Reward

Kelli called with some news that she said involved making some big decisions. My brain was scrambling with curiosity. I didn't know what the heck that meant, so I didn't want to speculate. We'd already made the decision that we wanted to leave, so I hoped she didn't propose anything about staying, because that wasn't going to happen.

"Hey, baby. What's up?"

"You are never going to believe this, but I have the opportunity of a lifetime. I have the opportunity to become a vice president of sales, but the only catch is that we have to move to Canada."

"Canada? Holy crap. I know we said we were going to move away, but I didn't consider leaving the country. Wow, congratulations, baby. That's awesome!"

"You mean you support me taking the job?"

"Of course I do."

She was so excited that she immediately started making our exit plans. I tuned her out as she was talking, because I started to get the sense of dread.

"Wait a minute, baby. Canada is kind of strict. You know I have a little bit of a sketchy background."

"No, you don't. All that was washed away when you got your pardon."

"Yes, that's right."

The whole purpose for the Lord blessing me with the pardon was not for me to get a job. It was because the Lord knew this opportunity for Kelli would come along. I received this pardon five years ago, and it has not benefited me in any way. The Lord has been planning this all along.

•••

The prospect of moving to Canada sounded good, but there was still the matter of selling my business. I was contacted by a turnkey investment firm that said they had a Japanese buyer prepared to make an offer on my entire thirty-seven-property portfolio at asking price without seeing the properties. That was preposterous. No one would spend that type of money without seeing the properties or having them inspected. The turnkey firm assured me the offer was legitimate and they would be taking over the management of the properties for the buyer. When something was too good to be true, then it probably was, so I was not holding my breath.

Under normal circumstances I would say that under Murphy's Law, anything that could go wrong, would go wrong. But I got a wire transfer for the entire amount into my bank account. *Thank You, God, I didn't see that coming!*

I'd listened to Warren Buffet in a sixty-second sound bite, and his advice had netted me the financial stability I could've only dreamed about. That was an unthinkable scenario. I was a nobody from the middle of nowhere. I didn't have a social media profile. I'd never voted. All my investments were in limited liability companies. The only thing that showed I existed was my criminal record, and now that was gone too. I was invisible, and I loved it. Kelli, Patience, and I were heading to a new land with no baggage behind us. I couldn't wait to see what the Lord had in store.

Step of Obedience

The three of us purchased a nice brick 3,800-square-foot house just outside of Toronto. It was not nearly as nice as our house in Ohio, but it was in a great community. It also cost about three times as much, but we didn't care. We were blessed and eager to start our new lives.

The people of Toronto were absolutely awesome. Everyone was very polite and welcoming. The food was even healthier, and the government paid for health care. Canada was really a diamond in the rough.

I was glad Toronto had satellite radio. That way I could still get my spiritual food from Pastor O. Since I'd started listening to him, I hadn't been able to turn him off. I heard many people who claimed to be men of God, but I can truly testify that the words from Pastor O were inspired by God Himself. There had never been a message he preached that didn't speak directly to things I was going through in my life. The one thing he said at the end of every message was to "get into a Bible-based church and put God in first place."

Maybe that was what I was missing. I honored God with my actions and my prayers, but I had never spent any time worshipping Him.

I searched on the internet for churches near me, and the very first one to pop up was the North Bible Chapel, only two blocks away. I checked out their website to ensure their doctrine matched up with what I believed. I decided to pay a visit, and once I walked in, I could feel the Holy Spirit's presence. The leader of the church was a man named Pastor Bob, a prolific speaker. He got so excited when he reached a critical part of his sermon that you couldn't help but get captured in his word. The first time I heard him speak, I couldn't help but cry. I'd prayed that the Lord would help me find His people before I went into the church. I didn't want to go to any church; I wanted to go where I could grow in faith.

I had been attending for a couple of months when Pastor Bob showed a video of people getting baptized. He followed the video with a scripture that spoke about baptism as an act of obedience for all believers. By taking that act of obedience, you showed you were accepting Christ as your Lord and Savior. I had never thought about the fact that I wasn't baptized, but I was eager to take this important step.

Before you could be baptized at North Bible Chapel, you had to fill out a declaration of what Christ meant to you and what He had done in your life. You would have to read your testimony out loud before the congregation. After you read it, you were submerged into the water to complete your baptism. I had never been so exhilarated for any event in my life. It would be the day I joined the Lord and washed myself clean of all my sin. I was more than ready!

On the day of my baptism, I couldn't be more nervous. I felt butterflies in my stomach, but I was eager to start my life anew. There were six people being baptized the same day, but I was going to be first. I changed into my swim trunks and stood in a single-file line at the entrance to the stage.

Once I walked through a curtain to step out in front of everyone, I felt a huge rush of wind. We were indoors, but it was as if I were standing outside on a blustery day. I went up three steps into a huge blue water tank. The water was warm, still, and just right. I moved forward to where Pastor Bob was waiting by a microphone.

Pastor Bob began to introduce me to the congregation, and that was when I looked up to see something I could not believe. The tank was on stage in front of thousands of people. I froze and began to tremble uncontrollably. It was something I'd said I would never do again: stand on stage in front of people. I'd shamed myself so bad many years ago and had made the decision that I would never set foot on a platform.

The Lord knew it. The Lord had never allowed me to realize that my declaration of faith would be on stage, because I never would've done it. It was too late to turn back. I grabbed my declaration page, pulled it to my face, and began to read through a face full of tears.

> "Before I knew Christ, I never had an opinion about religion. I just knew it wasn't for me. Growing up as a homeless teenager, I learned I couldn't depend on anyone but myself. I believed that every accolade and every accomplishment

Sleeping in the Jungle

was achieved by my education and my hard work. For fourteen out of my seventeen years of marriage, my wife has patiently and lovingly tried to lead me to Christ, but I could not see the benefits. I used the flaws and hypocrisy of those within the congregation as evidence that organized religion was for people who were brainwashed and totally separated from reality.

"I received Christ, like most people, when I reached the lowest point in my life. As I began to take an inventory of my life, I realized there is no way I could have accomplished all I have on my own. The Lord has breathed life into every aspect of my life and continuously sent Angels filled with the Holy Spirit to get me to recognize who really deserved the glory. I received Christ when I realized that He was with me even when I wasn't with Him. Even though I never considered myself to be a Christ follower, He knew I was. I take comfort in knowing that Jesus stood by my side, rescued me over and over again, rained His favor over me, and blessed me with His shield of protection, even if I never did anything to deserve it. I often ask Jesus why He has blessed me so much, and the only answer I get is that He knew one day I would be here. He knew one day I would be standing beside this tank. He knew I would take this step of obedience and allow Him to use me to further His kingdom!

"Now, with Christ in my life I not only trust Him, but I completely turn my life over to Him to lead me wherever He sees fit. I start every day by thanking Him for directing my footsteps, for filling my heart with His Holy Spirit, for bringing the right people into my life, and for the privilege to bless others in order to do His will. The reason why I have been so anxious to get baptized, the reason I am so excited for today, is because today is the day I finally get to tell Jehovah God and my beautiful wife, who are my reasons for living... 'Thank you for not giving up on me!'"

As soon as I was done reading, Pastor Bob immersed my entire body under the water. When I arose from the water, I heard a huge round of applause and admiration from the crowd.

That was the sound that kept me up at night. The sound of applause and the feeling of being on stage that I felt was missing from my life. My shame and fear of going on stage would never have allowed me to do it if the Lord had not guided me. It was boggling my mind that the Lord would choose the moment I'd turned my life over to Him to help me overcome my shame. *What does this mean? What is the Lord trying to tell me?*

Rocked Awake

I didn't know what the Lord was trying to tell me by guiding me back on stage. I could never return to a life of stand-up comedy because my reputation was far too damaged. Even if it weren't, the grind of trying to be discovered in stand-up was too grueling, and I was too far along in my life to start over again. The one thing I had never lost was my desire to make people laugh. I loved comedy so much, but I still feared the backlash of resurfacing again after so many years.

Although comedy was no longer my life, I still studied the great comedians and I loved to watch documentaries about them. I watched a comedy documentary on the great George Wallace and noticed they were doing an interview with Chris Rock.

George Wallace had been Chris Rock's mentor, and Chris noted that he would do anything to emulate George. Chris said that when he would catch George's performance in downtown New York, he would run to uptown New York and get on stage to tell the same jokes.

"Hey, that's what I did." I'd walked away from comedy in shame and had vowed never to return because of stealing people's jokes, but Chris Rock had done the same thing. There was no doubt that what we both had done was wrong, but when you were just starting out, there was a degree of grace that was given. They said that sometimes we were our own toughest critics, and we thought that other people had not forgiven us because we hadn't forgiven ourselves. Once again, God had sent an unlikely messenger to help turn me around, but if I had not heard Chris Rock say those words, I might have never forgiven myself for what I'd done. Even if I had the desire to take another stab at entertainment, where would I begin? I didn't know a soul in Canada. With zero connections and zero notoriety, I was years away from making people laugh again.

Hard to Say Goodbye

It was only two years after Stanley had achieved his dream of becoming a municipal court judge that he became gravely ill back in Ohio. He was in the hospital, but his secretary said he was asking for me. He'd been presiding over a routine day in court when he'd just collapsed. The paramedics said that his heart had stopped more than once, but just like the litigating fighter I knew, he was hanging in there.

I quickly rushed across the border to be by his side. Once I arrived at the hospital, I saw that it didn't look good.

Walking through the hospital always gave me the creeps, because all you smelled was rubbing alcohol. It would seem like smelling the place would make a patient sicker. I was glad he was in a room by himself so we could have an opportunity to talk.

I tried to creep in the door as silently as possible to keep from disturbing him because he appeared to be asleep. Why did they always have to make the hospital seem so dreary and plain? The walls were eggshell, the floor was eggshell, and he was only wearing half of a gown.

Sleeping in the Jungle

I was starting to feel sick, and I had just arrived. He was rolled up in several blankets with IVs and monitors connected to him everywhere. His long, skinny frame took up the entire length of the bed. He had both of his arms spread wide apart, lying motionless with his mouth wide open.

I slumped down in the seat next to his bed and whispered, "I know you're sick, but I know that you can hear me. Please don't die."

That was when I saw him slowly turn toward me. "Who in the hell said something about dying?"

Surprised by the response, I said, "Ain't nothing wrong with you, man. Why would you want to scare me like that?"

"I had to lay on the side like that. It gave things a more dramatic effect."

We both began to laugh. "Man, your secretary made it sound like you were about to check out."

"Well, she may have made it seem worse than it was, but I asked her to do that to make sure you came. I'm not outwardly sick, but I am very ill. I have an aggressive form of colon cancer, and they say there's not much they can do to fix me."

It felt like someone had dropped a ton of bricks on me. I'd come here thinking the worst. When we'd started talking and laughing, I'd thought it was all going to get better. Then I'd found out it was the worst all over again. "Naw, Stanley, don't say that, man." Tears began to flow from us both.

"Listen, don't worry about me, son. I have lived a great life. I just wanted to make sure I didn't leave this earth without saying a few things to you."

I fought to contain my grief. "What's on your mind, my brother?"

"I know you have had a roller coaster of a life and you have been hesitant to share it with people out of fear that they will judge you. I have witnessed the impact God has had on your life, and your story is one that could help a lot of young people who have grown up like you. If you tell the story the right way, I know you can be a *New York Times* bestseller. You can be an Oscar winner. All you have to do is embrace your destiny and stop running from it. Who cares what other people think? The story is not for people who will judge you, it's for the people you will inspire. Promise me you will tell your story."

Embracing Stanley, I made the vow. "I promise, my brother. I promise."

"Trust me, your story will manufacture inspiration!"

MGFIN
Manufacturing Inspiration

Three days later, Stanley was gone. I wasn't saddened by his passing, I was inspired. I would never forget my good friend. I had peace knowing he was in a better place, and I knew he would be an angel in heaven looking down and protecting his brother in Christ.

I'd given Stanley my word that I would tell my story, and I could never let him down. There was no need for me to be afraid or ashamed; it was time to get to work.

While I was in Ohio, I made a quick stop to see the three brothers. I hadn't seen them since our film had screened at the Cleveland Film Festival. I let them know I wanted to do another short film that told more of my story. I named my new film company in honor of my father figure and most influential mentor. He'd said my

SLEEPING IN THE JUNGLE

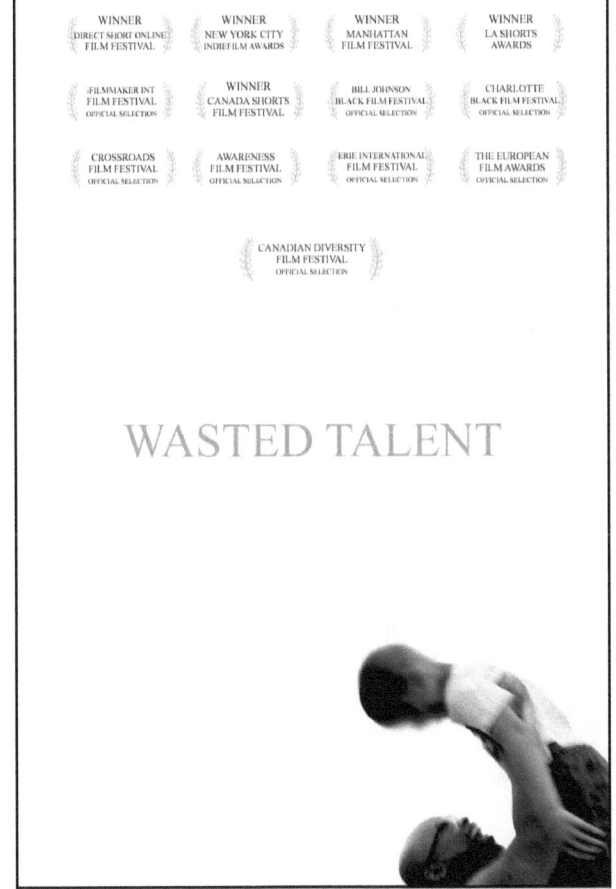

story would manufacture inspiration, and therefore the acronym MFGIN was born. It stood for Manufacturing Inspiration. The title of the second film would also honor the fallen. Jonesy's brother Lil' Nicky and Kelli's nephew Terrell had both left this world way too early, so I titled the film *Wasted Talent*.

INTERNATIONAL RECOGNITION

Wasted Talent was a huge success. It was winning awards in the US, Canada, and Europe. I could hardly believe the film was doing so well. It served as a sequel to the first film, *Sleeping in the Jungle*, and had the film world buzzing about what was going to happen in the next part. I played my father in both films, but I took a larger acting role in *Wasted Talent* because I wanted to make sure I conveyed how strong my father's love was for me.

My short films had also garnered some recognition in Canada. As a result, I'd made several industry connections. One of my connections told me about a casting call I should audition for. I auditioned for the role of a record producer named "Rock Crimson." I didn't think my face really said "Rock Crimson," but I gave it everything that I had.

I couldn't believe I got the part. I was really going to be on television. It was too much for me to comprehend. The sketch comedy show was about a zany celebrity interviewer named Sarah Trifano who always found herself in new adventures.

Jumbo TV, Yonge-Dundas Square in downtown Toronto

Sleeping in the Jungle

The premise for my character was introduced when a group of celebrity friends convinced her to make a song for a charity album, and she needed producer Rock Crimson's help. After three episodes, including the season finale, we finally got the song made. She had a nationwide viewership that reached 12.5 million viewers on a weekly basis. The crazy thing I never realized until I saw the show on TV was that every time I told a joke, it was on 12.5 million TV screens. I'd just made 12.5 million people laugh. My prayer to make people laugh again had been answered!

The Perfect Wine

There was a beautiful country music artist in Canada who went by the name Perfect Wine. She was becoming a huge celebrity, and people were anointing her as the next big thing. She had a new hit song called "Heartbreak Hotel." She was looking for someone to co-star in the video with her as a comedy relief who looked like the rapper Cee-Lo Green. I didn't think I looked like Cee-Lo, but I auditioned for the part anyway.

Apparently, Perfect Wine thought I looked like him, because I got the part without an audition. The photos and film footage were all she needed to see. The video depicted me as a rude hotel owner who didn't want kids partying in his establishment. I harassed the partygoers at every turn. Once I realized they were having too much fun and the women were so beautiful, I eventually joined the party. It was a feel-good country video for the whole family to laugh at. Once again, I was making people laugh on a nationwide scale.

Perfect Wine was nominated for the Canadian Country Music Artist of the year. She had the honor of performing on the award show, and she was actually going to perform the song. It was too good to be true and impossible to script. Only the Lord could launch me from the back of the line to the front of the line in an instant. *Thank You, God! I didn't see that coming!*

Sleeping in the Jungle

Perfect Wine video set

Salute to the World

I had a meeting with a talent agent who said he wanted to manage my acting career. Taft Ellington had worked with numerous actors and models from Canada. He gave me a huge list he'd made to build my new persona.

- A. Create a photo shoot and marketing campaign
- B. Build a viral internet presence
- C. Flood all social media platforms with your background
- D. Solicit roles in high-profile productions
- E. Start working on night club and radio appearances

Sleeping in the Jungle

I took the list home and realized that all the things on the list were things I didn't want to do. When I was a young immature man, I'd fallen in love with making people laugh. When I couldn't have it anymore, I thought I would never be happy without it. Since I had grown older and wiser, I had fallen in love with other things. I loved traveling with Kelli and Patience. I loved cooking dinner for them every night. I also loved being separated from the world. I would go so far as to say that I loved all those things more than I loved making people laugh.

I promised Stanley Vegetarian that I would tell my story, and that was all the notoriety I wanted. Whether my story moved one person or a million, that was the only spotlight I was looking for. I can confidently say I was right at the plateau of fame and I didn't want it. Everyone else could have the world, and I saluted those who embraced it. As for me, I just wanted to go back to being invisible.

Forgiveness

I have done a lot of things in my life I am not proud of. I hurt people both directly and indirectly with my words and actions. For that, I truly apologize and pray for their forgiveness. To everyone who has ever harmed me, either directly or indirectly, I need you to know that I forgive you. If I believe the Lord has directed my footsteps, then it was ordained for us to hurt each other. Whatever the motive is for the Lord to allow the hurt to take place, I know it was meant for our journey. It helped us grow, helped us persevere, showed us how to survive in the darkest valleys, gave us determination, and gave us fuel.

•••

It took a long time for my faith to bring me to the place where I am now. It had been almost twenty-five years since my father's murder, and most of the killers were up for parole. Two months ago, I went to a parole hearing for Cat. Although she was the person who'd set my father up to be murdered, I acknowledged that my dad had done some horrible things to her as well. In no way was I excusing her actions, but thirty years later, I believed she had paid dearly for her crimes and deserved an opportunity to be free. Her parents, children, and siblings had been praying for years that they would see her free one day, and for that, I laid down my pain. I told the parole board that I forgave her and I hoped she forgave my dad. I prayed God would bless her and that she lived the best life. If there was anything I could do to help her get on her feet, I would gladly help.

My words must have hit their mark, because by the grace of God, Cat was being released from prison. I knew it would be inappropriate for me to be there, but I couldn't resist the opportunity to witness her release. I drove out to the prison and slumped down in the driver's seat of my car. The female prison looked just as menacing as the male prison. Huge red brick buildings surrounded by fence and barbed wire as far as the eye could see. I parked a safe distance away but close enough so I could see her family as they awaited her release. They were lined up outside with balloons and posters. This was as picturesque as a movie. When the doors opened and she ran out, all you could see was hysteria. They were cheering and hugging so much that I couldn't see what she looked like. As they made their way to the white van awaiting the entourage, I still had not even gotten a glimpse of her. I hoped I hadn't driven all the way out there for nothing. I should have brought some binoculars. *Come on, Lord, let me just get a peek? I should have parked closer.*

Just as everyone loaded up, Cat walked back away from the van, looked up in the sky, and took a deep breath. As she did so, I had a perfect view of her. She was just as short as I remembered. The twenty-five years of imprisonment had not been generous to her frame, but she wasn't overweight. She looked like an average middle-aged woman. I wasn't slumped in the car anymore; my body was leaning forward as I tried to see as much as I could. When they drove off, I thought, *Did she come out to take that deep breath and look up at the sky because she was thanking God for answering her prayers? Did the forgiveness and mercy I showed her help God answer her prayer? Mercy and grace are something none of us deserve, but we get blessed with it every day. I wish her the greatest life and I will do everything in my power to make sure the other killers get a fair shot at freedom as well.*

WHERE WERE YOU?

Where were you when you realized you had the Lord's favor on your life? Where were you when you realized the Lord had directed your footsteps and planned your entire life? I knew where I was. I was writing this story when it hit me.

Did the Lord allow me to fall ill so I could avoid being killed in the house with my father? Did He allow me to be arrested in a stolen car so I could be rescued from sleeping in the Jungle Gym? Did He send Black to provide a means for me to earn a living and provide support for my daughter? Did the Lord send the Jerk to snitch on me to push me out of the drug lifestyle?

When I was certain to serve a lengthy jail sentence, did the Lord send an angel named Queen Mother to intervene? Did He send me the best lawyer in Stanley Vegetarian to free me from that lengthy jail sentence? Was Kelli an angel? Did He allow the most beautiful woman in the world to see me as someone she wanted to meet, love, and spend the rest of her life with? Did the Lord use Steel Shot to build my work ethic, and then ultimately have me fired so I could be pushed into my destiny? Did He bless me with supernatural comprehension so I could stand out in school and achieve scholastic honors with little effort? Did the Lord arrange my graduation days before my mother's death so that we could heal and have closure?

Did the Lord use Warren Buffet to give me advice on providing for my family, knowing I would soon be without a job? Did the Lord use my story of desperation, perseverance, and determination to inspire the governor to pardon me and restore my honor? Did He send Stanley Vegetarian to mentor me and help me to become a better man to become a productive member of society?

Did the Lord send an angel investor to buy me out of my real estate business right before it began to crumble? Was it the Lord who stopped Black's gun as he was about to take my life? Did He use the governor's pardon as a means for me to leave the country and live a life free from danger?

Did the Lord use Ice Cube to inspire me and provide direction on how to make movies? Did God use Chris Rock to show me I didn't have to be ashamed to go on stage and perform again?

Let's put this into perspective. Did God Almighty himself give me this insane story so I could write about it, write about Him? Give Him the glory? I want you to consider the unthinkable. What if the Lord gave me this story and used all these people to inspire *YOU*? My faith allowed me to believe that none of these things happened by accident. I truly have faith that all those situations and people were used to get me to this moment, because God loves me that much!

The Almighty is using us all for one purpose, to bring honor and glory to His name. No matter how bad you think you have had it in your life, if you're willing to give Him the glory for every achievement, you too can achieve supernatural things. If this book inspires you to look over your life and recognize the provisions that He has made for you, His will has been done. If it inspires you to turn your life over to Him, His will has been done. If this book moves you in any way toward the glory of God, then He inspired me to write this book for you, BECAUSE HE LOVES YOU THAT MUCH!

KING DAVID

King David of the Holy Bible learned early on in life that God was to be trusted and obeyed. David's faith pleased God, and God rewarded him for his faithfulness. His life was a true example of success and failure, and the Bible illustrates he was far from perfect. What elevated David above the rest was that his heart was pointed toward God, even when he did wrong. David was a man after God's own heart in that he was thankful (Acts 13:22). "I wash my hands in innocence, and go about your altar, O LORD, proclaiming aloud your praise and telling of all your wonderful deeds" (Psalm 26:6–7).

WHY IS THE TRUTH IN ME?

After a lifetime of trying to figure out who I am, I finally have the answer. I am an unlikely messenger just like many of the people I perceived as unlikely messengers. In the Bible, the Israelites didn't make it into the promised land because they got comfortable where they were. My mom told me I was destined to be king, but I didn't believe and opted for a comfortable life. I was satisfied being a highly favored man whom God answers his prayers. Once I realized He is not only the hearer of my prayers but the deliverer of my prayers, I wondered what I could do with such favor and provision. What if I was bold enough to pray that I could become king? Could I have had the throne?

What fool would want to become a king in this wicked system knowing the Lord's wrath is upon us? How can I hunger for promotion in this world, knowing its fate? I wish that I was not burdened with the truth. Why do I see that when Jerusalem was named Israel's territory, Israel was in control of the ground of the New Covenant; the ransom sacrifice; the reason we can live forever; the one Christians claim to love? Why do I see that Israel is charging a tax on the church that houses Jesus' tomb? Why do I see the tax collectors as they came to the resting place where Jesus arose from the dead? Why do I see the wicked plan to exact revenge on Jesus Christ, His family, and many heroes of faith? Why do I see how it all is going to end? Why me? Why has God burdened me with these visions?

Why am I the only one who sees God's wrath coming like a black hole swallowing everything in its path? Who would want to be the king of this? I know that the Lord will answer any prayer that I pray, and I could easily pray for what my mom saw in me; my father saw in me; my mentors saw in me; what God saw in me. I could pray for greatness and receive it. Although I could pray for that, I would rather pray for you. I would like to have my greatest prayer be that the merciful God Jehovah gives mankind another chance. I pray that He halts His wrath and gives us another chance to love each other as He loves us. I ask that He softens the hearts of those who are looking to murder, oppress and destroy us all for power. No matter if you believe that Jesus was the Son of God or not, everyone believes at minimum that He was a prophet who was favored by God. How could you receive that information and not halt everything that you are involved in? Jesus Christ himself deserves your praise. Are you willing to say that you hate anything more than you love Jesus?

Now that the devil knows his time is short, he simply wants to see how many people he can take with him. In the biblical story of Job, the devil had to ask for permission to test Job. If you love the Lord, the wicked one must also ask for permission to test you. Is there anything that you are doing that you can't defend if Jesus was standing in front of you? When Jesus was dying on the cross He yelled out, "Forgive them for they know not what they do" (Luke 23:34). On the day of the end you will not have the luxury of that statement. You know exactly who the Lord is, and you know exactly what is happening, but you hate more than you love.

Our Lord is upon us right now, but He is so merciful that He has given us a way out and He has trusted me to use my voice and be a messenger. I have no idea why He would choose a wretch like me, but He has. It turns out you had the information all along. We can halt the Lord's wrath if we do three simple things:

1. Accept Jesus Christ as your Lord and Savior (Romans 10:13).
2. Get baptized in water into Jesus Christ's Kingdom (I Peter 3:21).
3. The final and easiest requirement of all: You have to love everything that you hate…

1 JOHN 2:9-11. ⁹Anyone who claims to be in the light but hates a brother or sister is still in the darkness. ¹⁰Anyone who loves their brother and sister lives in the light, and there is nothing in them to make them stumble. ¹¹But anyone who hates a brother or sister is in the darkness and walks around in the darkness. They do not know where they are going, because the darkness has blinded them.

1 JOHN 2:15-17. ¹⁵Do not love the world or anything in the world. If anyone loves the world, love for the Father is not in them. ¹⁶For everything in the world—the lust of the flesh, the lust of the eyes, and the pride of life—comes not from the Father but from the world. ¹⁷The world and its desires pass away, but whoever does the will of God lives forever.